I0201831

What's the Matter?

A New Shakespeare Play

by

A. K. Ludwig

Shakespeare Publications
Berkeley, California

Copyright © 2014 by A. K. Ludwig

All rights reserved. Published by arrangement
with the author. The material contained herein is
for the personal use of the reader and may not be
performed or incorporated in any commercial
programs or other books, databases, or any other
kind of software without the written permission of
the publisher or author. Making copies of this
book, or any portion of it, for any purpose other
than your own, is a violation of United States
copyright laws.

Theatrical companies interested in an abridged
version of this work, may request a free digital
copy (PDF) in play manuscript format at
Shakespeare-Publications.com.

Published by
Shakespeare Publications
Berkeley, California

ISBN-13: 978-0-615-95372-4

For Dorothy

What's the Matter?

CHARACTERS

SICILIANS

Katrina	Princess of Sicily
Amadeo	Prince of Sicily
Lucentio	King of Sicily, father of Amadeo and Katrina
Adrianna	Queen of Sicily, mother of Amadeo and Katrina
Camillo	Duke of Syracuse, brother-in-law of Lucentio
Morelli	Duke of Messina, brother of Lucentio
Sophia	Wife of Amadeo
Lucinda	Daughter of Morelli, cousin and confidant of Katrina
Duchess	Duchess of Messina, wife of Morelli
First Lord	
Second Lord	
Perfumo	Sicilian soldier
Rinaldo	Sicilian soldier
Mistress Closet	Proprietor of tavern in Palermo

Ladies, Attendants, Messengers, Captains, Townspeople

BURGUNDIANS

Valmond	Duke of Burgundy
Beauchance	Count of Provence, his companion, suitor of Lucinda
Monsieur Musik	Frenchman in service to Valmond
Pierre	Companion of Musik
Captains	

NEAPOLITANS

Cosimo	Prince of Naples
Tertius	Lord and counselor to Prince
Cambio	Prince's underling and instrument
Captains	

Soldiers of Sicily, Burgundy, and Naples; Royal Attendants

SETTING

Sicily and Burgundy

ACT I

Scene 1

Palermo. Hall of royal palace. Enter Lucinda, Katrina, and Sophia.

Lucinda. Love is a spirit all compact of fire,
　　Not gross to sink, but light, and will aspire.

Katrina. Coz, I have heard it is a life in death,
　　That laughs and weeps, and all but with a breath.

Sophia. Lucinda, tell this maid what 'tis to love.

Lucinda. It is to be all made of sighs and tears.

Sophia. It is to be all made of faith and service.

Lucinda. It is to be all made of fantasy.

Sophia. All adoration, duty, and respect.

Lucinda. All made of passion and all made of wishes.

Sophia. All humbleness, all patience and impatience,
　　All purity, all trial, all observance.

Katrina. Love, Sophia, is all wanton as a child,
　　That longs for every thing that he can come by;
　　Full of unbefitting strains, skipping and vain,
　　Formed by the eye and therefore, like the eye,
　　Full of strange shapes, of habits and of forms,
　　Varying in subjects as the eye doth roll
　　To every varied object in his glance.

Lucinda. Love is a smoke raised with the fume of sighs;
　　Being purged, a fire sparkling in lovers' eyes;
　　Being vex'd a sea nourish'd with lovers' tears:
　　What is it else?

Katrina. Love, dear ladies, is merely a madness—

Sophia. —A madness most discreet.

Katrina. Love is merely a madness, and, I tell you,
  deserves as well a dark house and a whip as madmen
  do: and the reason why they are not so punished and
  cured is, that the lunacy is so ordinary that the
  whippers are in love too. This driveling love is like a
  great natural, that runs lolling up and down to hide his
  bauble in a hole.

Lucinda. This is the montruosity in love, Katrina: the will
  is infinite and the execution confined, the desire is
  boundless and the act a slave to limit.

Katrina. To be wise and love exceeds man's might.
  All this wooing, wedding, and repenting, is as a Scotch
  jig, a measure, and a cinque pace: the first suit is hot
  and hasty, like a Scotch jig, and full as fantastical; the
  wedding, mannerly-modest, as a measure, full of state
  and ancientry; and then comes repentance and, with
  his bad legs, falls into the cinque pace faster and
  faster, till he sink into his grave. And men are April
  when they woo, December when they wed: maids are
  May when they are maids, but the sky changes when
  they are wives.

Sophia. Still, Princess, I hope to see you one day fitted
  with a husband.

Katrina. Not till God make men of some other metal than
  earth. Would it not grieve a woman to be
  overmastered with a piece of valiant dust? to make an
  account of her life to a clod of wayward marl?

Sophia. Thy husband is thy lord, thy life, thy keeper,
  And craves no other tribute at thy hands
  But love, fair looks and true obedience;
  Too little payment for so great a debt.

Such duty as the subject owes the prince
Even such a woman oweth to her husband.

Katrina. No, Sophia, I'll none: Adam's sons are my
brethren; and, truly, I hold it a sin to match in my
kindred. Besides, I could not endure a husband with a
beard on his face: I had rather lie in the woolen. He
that hath a beard is more than a youth, and he that
hath no beard is less than a man: and he that is more
than a youth is not for me, and he that is less than a
man, I am not for him.
Returns from hunting now thy lord, thy keeper,
Thy noble husband, Prince Amadeo.

Enter Amadeo, Valmond, Beauchance, and Musik.

Sophia. With all our guests: Duke Valmond, Count
Beauchance,
And Monsieur Musik. Welcome visitors.

Amadeo. What's the matter, ladies?

Lucinda. Love.

Beauchance. Love! Than whom no mortal so
magnificent!

Musik. This whimpled, whining, purblind, wayward
boy;
This senior-junior, giant-dwarf, Dan Cupid;
Regent of love-rhymes, lord of folded arms,
The anointed sovereign of sighs and groans,
Liege of all loiterers and malcontents,
Dread prince of plackets, king of codpieces,
Sole imperator and great general
Of trotting 'paritors.

Beauchance. Ah, to be in love!

Musik. Where scorn is bought with groans;
Coy looks with heart-sore sighs; one fading

       moment's mirth
       With twenty watchful, weary, tedious nights:
       If haply won, perhaps a hapless gain;
       If lost, why then a grievous labour won;
       However, but a folly bought with wit,
       Or else a wit by folly vanquished.

Beauchance. So by your circumstance, you call me fool.
       'Tis love you cavil at: I am not Love.

Musik. Love is your master, for he masters you:
       And he that is so yoked by a fool,
       Methinks, should not be chronicled for wise.

Beauchance. Yet, Monsieur Musik, writers say, eating
           love
       Inhabits in the finest wits of all.

Musik. And writers say, by love the young and tender
           wit
       Is turn'd to folly.
       But wherefore waste I time to counsel thee,
       That art a votary to fond desire?

Katrina. Then counsel me, sir, if it please you.

Musik. Note this, sweet Princess Katrina:
       Where Love reigns, disturbing Jealousy
       Doth call himself Affection's sentinel;
       Gives false alarms, suggesteth mutiny,
       And in a peaceful hour doth cry "Kill, kill!"
       Distempering gentle Love in his desire,
       As air and water do abate the fire.
       And even as one heat another heat expels,
       Or as one nail by strength drives out another,
       So the remembrance of a former love
       Is by a newer object quite forgotten.

Beauchance. (*Gazing at Lucinda.*)
       O spirit of love! how quick and fresh art thou!

Musik. That falls into abatement and low price,
    Even in a minute.

Katrina. Alas, how love can trifle with itself.
    'Tis pity love should be so contrary.

Beauchance. Ay me! for aught that I could ever read,
    Could ever hear by tale or history,
    The course of true love—

Lucinda. Never did run smooth?

Beauchance. But, either it was different in blood—

Lucinda. O cross! too high to be enthrall'd to low.

Beauchance. Or else misgraffed in respect of years—

Lucinda. O spite! too old to be engaged to young.

Beauchance. Or else it stood upon the choice of
    friends—

Lucinda. O hell! to choose love by another's eyes.

Beauchance. Or, if there were a sympathy in choice,
    War, death, or sickness did lay siege to it,
    Making it momentary as a sound,
    Swift as a shadow, short as any dream;
    Brief as the lightning in the collied night,
    That, in a spleen, unfolds both heaven and earth,
    And ere a man hath power to say "Behold!"
    The jaws of darkness do devour it up.

Katrina. So quick bright things come to confusion.

Amadeo. These violent delights have violent ends
    And in their triumph die, like fire and powder,
    Which as they kiss consume: the sweetest honey
    Is loathsome in his own deliciousness
    And in the taste confounds the appetite:
    Therefore love moderately;

(*Putting his arm around wife Sophia.*)
Long love doth so;
Too swift arrives as tardy as too slow.

Sophia. What think'st thou, Duke Valmond?

Valmond. I know love is begun by time;
And I see, in passages of proof,
Time qualifies the spark and fire of it.
There lives within the very flame of love
A kind of wick or snuff that will abate it.

Sophia. Nay, my gentle duke; one day thou shalt find
Love's gentle spring doth always fresh remain.

Valmond. This word "love," which graybeards call divine,
Be resident in men like one another
And not in me.

Lucinda. O hard-believing love.

Musik. (*To Katrina, Lucinda, Sophia, and Amadeo.*)
He is of a very melancholy disposition.

Katrina. Wherefore?

Musik. What it should be,
More than his father's death, that thus hath put him
So much from th' understanding of himself,
I cannot dream of.
Was ever son so rued a father's death?
But thus far can I praise him; he is of a noble
Strain, of approved valour and confirmed honesty.
Hear him debate of commonwealth affairs,
You would say it hath been all in all his study:
Turn him to any cause of policy,
The Gordian knot of it he will unloose,
Familiar as his garter.

Amadeo. I will vouch the truth of this.

Musik. A true knight,

Not yet mature, yet matchless, firm of word,
Speaking in deeds and deedless in his tongue;
Not soon provoked nor being provoked soon calm'd:
His heart and hand both open and both free;
For what he has he gives, what thinks he shows;
Yet gives he not till judgment guide his bounty,
Nor dignifies an impure thought with breath.

Amadeo. The duke looks cheerfully and smooth today;
He hath a kind of honour sets him off.
I think there's never a man in Christendom
That can less hide his love or hate than he;
For by his face straight shall you know his heart.

Amadeo leads Sophia and Katrina over to Valmond.

Amadeo. Sister, thou rememberest the Duke of
         Burgundy,
And know'st that we two went to school together.

Valmond. We were trained together in our childhoods.
In school-days' friendship, childhood innocence,
We, like two artificial gods,
Had been incorporate and grew together,
So, with two seeming bodies, but one heart.

Amadeo. There rooted betwixt us then such an affection,
which cannot choose but branch now. Since our more
mature dignities and royal necessities make separation
of our society, our encounters, though not personal,
have been royally attorneyed with interchange of gifts,
letters, loving embassies; we have seemed to be
together, though absent, shook hands, as over a vast,
and embraced, as it were, from the ends of opposed
winds.

Katrina. The heavens continue your loves. I think, this
coming summer, my brother means to pay
Burgundy the visitation which he justly owes him.

Amadeo. School days! Frightful, desperate, wild, and
    furious,
    Our prime of manhood daring, bold, and venturous.
    Nay, I remember the trick you served me when—

Sophia. (*To Katrina, cutting off Amadeo.*)
    Be kind and courteous to this gentleman.

          Sophia leads Amadeo away.

Katrina. Sir, I have seen you in the court of France.

Valmond. I have been sometimes there.

Katrina. They say you are a melancholy fellow.

Valmond. I am so, Princess. I myself am best
    When least in company.

Katrina. But wherefore? What's the matter, sir?

Valmond. I have of late lost all my mirth;
    In sooth, I know not why I am so sad:
    It wearies me;
    But how I caught it, found it, or came by it,
    What stuff 'tis made of, whereof it is born,
    I am to learn;
    And such a want-wit sadness makes of me,
    That I have much ado to know myself.

Katrina. Perhaps the remembrance of thy father's death?

Valmond. I prithee, Princess Katrina,
    Measure my strangeness with my unripe years:
    Before I know myself, seek not to know me.

Katrina. Pardon me. Then let us say you are sad
    Because you are not merry: I trust that you
    Be not one of such vinegar aspect
    That they'll not show their teeth in way of smile,
    Though Nestor swear the jest be laughable.

Valmond. I cannot hide what I am; I must be sad when I
    have cause, eat when I have stomach and laugh when I
    am merry. I hold the world but as
    A stage where every man must play a part
    And mine a sad one.

Katrina. The more pity.
        (*Gesturing toward Beauchance and Lucinda.*)
    But here is a pair of loving turtle-doves.

Valmond. Love's firm votary.

Katrina. And Love's high priestess.
    At the first sight they have changed eyes.
    There was never any thing so sudden—no sooner
    met but they looked—

Valmond. No sooner looked but they loved—

Katrina. No sooner loved but they sighed—

Valmond. No sooner sighed but they asked one another
    the reason—

Katrina. No sooner knew the reason but they sought the
    remedy—

Valmond. And in these degrees they have made a pair of
    stairs which they will climb incontinent—

Katrina. Or else be incontinent before marriage: they are
    in the very wrath of love and they will together.

Valmond. I do know the Count a well-accomplished
        youth,
    Of all that virtue love for virtue loved:
    For he hath wit to make an ill shape good.

Katrina. And shape to win grace though he had no wit.

Valmond. And a merrier man,
    Within the limit of becoming mirth,

I never spent an hour's talk withal:
His eye begets occasion for his wit;
For every object that the one doth catch
The other turns to a mirth-moving jest,
Which his fair tongue, conceit's expositor,
Delivers in such apt and gracious words
That aged ears play truant at his tales
And younger hearings are quite ravished;
So sweet and voluble is his discourse.

Beauchance. (*To Lucinda.*) Sweet maid,
Dost thou think that the oath of a lover
Is no stronger than the word of a tapster?

Lucinda. Do you question me, as an honest man should
do, for my simple true judgment; or would you have
me speak after my custom, as being a professed tyrant
to their sex?

Beauchance. I pray thee speak in sober judgment.

Lucinda. I think oaths are servants to deceitful men.

Beauchance. 'Tis not the many oaths that makes the
truth,
But the plain single vow that is vow'd true.
And thy fair virtue's force perforce doth move me
On the first view to say, to swear, I love thee.
I will live in thy heart, die in thy lap, and be
buried in thy eyes.

Lucinda. For your verity in love, I do think you as concave
as a covered goblet or a worm-eaten nut. I thank God
and my cold blood: I had rather hear my dog bark at a
crow than a man swear he loves me.

Beauchance. Lady, you are the cruell'st she alive,
If you will lead these graces to the grave
And leave the world no copy.

Lucinda.   O, sir, I will not be so hard-hearted; I will give
      out divers schedules of my beauty: it shall be
      inventoried, and every particle and utensil labeled to
      my will: as, item, two lips, indifferent red; item, two
      blue eyes, with lids to them; item, one neck, one chin,
      and so forth.

Beauchance.   I see you what you are, you are too proud;
      But, if you were the devil, you are fair.

Lucinda.   Is it not true that young men's love then lies
      Not truly in their hearts, but in their eyes?

Beauchance.   Then, I confess.
      Mine eye is much enthralled to thy shape;
      So is mine ear enamour'd of thy note.
      Did my heart love till now? forswear it, sight!
      For I never saw true beauty till this night.

      Enter King Lucentio and Queen Adrianna, attended.

Amadeo.   It is the Duke of Burgundy, good father;
      And the Duke's companions in travel,
      Count Guy de Beauchance and Monsieur Musik.

Lucentio.   Most dearly welcome! The blessed gods
      Purge all infection from our air whilst you
      Do climate here!
      Give them friendly welcome every one:
      Let them want nothing that our house affords.
      Duke, thou bear'st thy father's face;
      Frank nature, rather curious than in haste,
      Hath well composed thee. Thy father's moral parts
      Mayst thou inherit too, and succeed thy father
      In manners, as in shape. Thy blood and virtue
      Contend for empire in thee, and thy goodness
      Share with thy birthright! Welcome to Palermo.

Valmond.   King Lucentio, Queen Adrianna,
      I offer greetings to thy royal person;
      My thanks and duty are your majesties'.

Lucentio. Our daughter Katrina
        Stands here, like beauty's child, whom nature gat
        For men to see, and seeing wonder at.

Katrina. It pleaseth you, my royal father, to express
        My commendations great, whose merit's less.

                        Enter Duke Camillo.

Lucentio. Know you our trusty brother-in-law,
        Lord Camillo, the Duke of Syracuse?

Valmond. Good Lord Camillo, health and fair greeting;
        Please let our old acquaintance be renewed.

Camillo. Excellent young man! We joy to see thee.
        And pardon us the interruption, Duke.
                        (*To Lucentio.*)
        I beseech your highness, pardon me; I have
        News to tell you. Here comes in embassy
        Lord Tertius of Naples, with yourself to speak.
        He attendeth here hard by,
        To know whether you'll admit him.
        Shall I call in the ambassador, my liege?

Lucentio. Not yet, my brother; we would be resolved,
        Before we hear him, of some things of weight
        That task our thoughts. Another day,
        After our guests God grants a fair departure,
        We will give him audience. In the meantime,
        Convey our greetings and provide for them.
                        (*To everyone.*)
        Come, come: let's to dinner, let's to dinner.

                        Exit All.

ACT I

Scene 2

Palermo. Garden of the royal palace. Lucinda and Beauchance, Katrina and Valmond, each couple strolling together.

Beauchance. Although I did meet thee but so late ago,
    Hear my soul speak:
    The very instant that I saw you, did
    My heart fly to your service; there resides,
    To make me slave to it;
    Being your slave, what should I do but tend
    Upon the hours and times of your desire?

Lucinda. Do you love me?
    If thou dost love, pronounce it faithfully.

Beauchance. O heaven, O earth, bear witness to this
        sound
    And crown what I profess with kind event
    If I speak true! if hollowly, invert
    What best is boded me to mischief! I
    Beyond all limit of what else i' the world
    Do love, prize, honour you.

Lucinda. If thou think'st I am too quickly won,
    I'll frown and be perverse and say thee nay,
    So thou wilt woo; but else, not for the world.
    In truth, fair Beauchance, I am too fond,
    And therefore thou mayst think my 'havior light:
    But trust me, gentleman, I'll prove more true
    Than those that have more cunning to be strange.
    I should have been more strange; therefore pardon
        me,
    And not impute this yielding to light love.

Beauchance. O Lucinda! Full many a lady
      I have eyed with best regard and many a time
      The harmony of their tongues hath into bondage
      Brought my too diligent ear: for several virtues
      Have I liked several women; never any
      With so fun soul, but some defect in her
      Did quarrel with the noblest grace she owed
      And put it to the foil: but you, O you,
      So perfect and so peerless, are created
      Of every creature's best! Wherefore weep you?

Lucinda. At mine unworthiness that dare not offer
      What I desire to give, and much less take
      What I shall die to want.
      Sweet, bid me hold my tongue,
      For in this rapture I shall surely speak
      The thing I shall repent.
      Thou know'st no less but all; I have unclasp'd
      To thee the book even of my secret soul.

Beauchance. What shall you ask of me that I'll deny?

Lucinda. The exchange of thy love's faithful vow for mine.

              Beauchance and Lucinda walk aside.

Valmond. Monsieur Musik is magnanimous;
      Of very reverend reputation,
      Of credit infinite, gentle, never schooled and yet
      learned, full of noble device, of all sorts enchantingly
      beloved; and a man that I love and honour with my
      soul, and my heart, and my duty, and my life.

Katrina. A fit counselor and servant for a prince.

Valmond. Full often he hath in conversation
      Told the sad story of my father's death,
      And twenty times made pause to sob and weep,
      That all the standers-by had wet their cheeks
      Like trees bedash'd with rain: in that sad time
      My manly eyes did scorn an humble tear.

Katrina. 'Tis sweet and commendable in his nature,
    To give these mourning duties to your father.
    But this makes you sad.

Valmond. Princess, if I have veil'd my look,
    I turn the trouble of my countenance
    Merely upon myself.

Katrina. I beg thy pardon, Duke.

Valmond. Trouble yourself no further. Vexed I am
    Of late with passions of some difference,
    Conceptions only proper to myself,
    Which give some soil perhaps to my behaviors;
    But let not therefore my good friends be grieved.
    I will from henceforth be of better cheer.

Katrina. I pray God's blessing into thy attempt.

Valmond. Princess, I thank thee for thy orisons.
    But yet methinks
    Our remedies oft in ourselves do lie,
    Which we ascribe to heaven.

Katrina. We cannot but obey the powers above us.

Valmond. The fated sky
    Gives us free scope, only doth backward pull
    Our slow designs when we ourselves are dull.

Katrina. What can be avoided
    Whose end is purposed by almighty God?

Valmond. Yet I will believe that
    What's to come is in your and my discharge.

Katrina. But there's a divinity that shapes our ends.

Valmond. In despite of all, Princess, I will live
    As if a man were author of himself.

       Enter Morelli and the Duchess of Messina.

Katrina. Look, here comes the Duke, my Uncle Morelli,
            And the Duchess, with eyes full of anger;
            He is a villain with a smiling cheek,
            A goodly apple rotten at the heart:
            O, what a goodly outside falsehood hath!

Morelli. (*Seeing Lucinda and Beauchance.*)
            To be paddling palms and pinching fingers,
            As now they are, and making practised smiles,
            As in a looking-glass, and then to sigh, as 'twere
            The mort o' the deer; O, that is entertainment
            My bosom likes not, nor my brows!

Valmond. Count Beauchance, let us depart, I pray you.

                    Exit Beauchance and Valmond.

Duchess. How now, daughter and our royal cousin:
            Beware of them, their promises, enticements, oaths,
            tokens, and all these engines of lust, are not the things
            they go under: many a maid hath been seduced by
            them. I hope I need not to advise you further; but I
            hope your own grace will keep you where you are,
            though there were no further danger known but the
            modesty which is so lost.

Morelli. Do not give dalliance
            Too much the rein: be more abstemious.

                    Exit Morelli and Duchess of Messina.

Lucinda. Tell me truly, coz, what thou think'st of
            Gentle County Beauchance.

Katrina. Truly, I have not seen
            So likely an ambassador of love;
            A day in April never came so sweet,
            To show how costly summer was at hand,
            As this fore-spurrer comes before his lord.
            Now, tell me, dost thou affect the Count?

Lucinda. How I dote on him! I do adore him so!
    Yea, I will hereupon confess—I am in love!

Katrina. Why he more than another?

Lucinda. Of many good I think him best.

Katrina. Your reason?

Lucinda. I have no other but a woman's reason; I think
    him so because I think him so.

Katrina. Is it possible, on such a sudden, you should fall
    into so strong a liking?

Lucinda. Yea, for soothe!
    Not mine own fears, nor the prophetic soul
    Of the wide world dreaming on things to come,
    Can yet the lease of my true love control!

Exit Lucinda.

Katrina. Even so quickly may one catch the plague?

Exit. Blackout.

ACT I

Scene 3

Palermo. Tavern. Musik and Pierre seated among other Patrons. Enter Perfumo and Rinaldo.

Perfumo. Salutation and greeting to you all!
    Monsieur Musik. Monsieur Pierre.

Musik. Signior Perfumo. Good day to you.
    Who is your companion now?

Rinaldo. Signior Rinaldo, sir, at your service.

Perfumo. A trusty villain, sir, that very oft,
    When I am dull with care and melancholy,
    Lightens my humour with his merry jests.
    Full of ambition, the soldier's virtue,
    Come haply to wive and thrive in Sicily.
    Though virtue is of so little regard in these
    costermonger times that true valour is turned bear-
    herd: pregnancy is made a tapster, and hath his quick
    wit wasted in giving reckonings: all the other gifts
    appertinent to man, as the malice of this age shapes
    them, are not worth a gooseberry. You that are old
    consider not the capacities of us that are young; you do
    measure the heat of our livers with the bitterness of
    your galls: and we that are in the vaward of our youth,
    I must confess, are wags too.

Musik. Wisdom cries out in the streets, and no man
    regards it.

Pierre. Where did you study all this goodly speech?

Perfumo. It is extempore, from my mother-wit. A gift that
    I have, simple, simple; a foolish extravagant spirit, full
    of forms, figures, shapes, objects, ideas,

apprehensions, motions, revolutions: these are begot
in the ventricle of memory, nourished in the womb of
pia mater, and delivered upon the mellowing of
occasion. But the gift is good in those in whom it is
acute, and I am thankful for it.

Patrons. Well said.

Perfumo. I love not many words.

Pierre. No more than a fish loves water.

Musik. Perfumo speaks an infinite deal of nothing, more
than any man in all Palermo. His reasons are as two
grains of wheat hid in two bushels of chaff: you shall
seek all day ere you find them, and when you have
them, they are not worth the search.

Perfumo. This is not generous, not gentle, not humble.

Musik. Fare thee well; fare thee well;
We hold our time too precious to be spent
With such a brabbler.

Exit Musik and Pierre.

Perfumo. I do not know the man I should avoid
So soon as that mocking Monsieur Musik.
Oh, I know him well. He reads much;
He is a great observer and he looks
Quite through the deeds of men: he loves no plays,
As thou dost, Rinaldo; he hears no music;
Seldom he smiles, and smiles in such a sort
As if he mock'd himself and scorn'd his spirit.
Holy Monsieur Musik scarce confesses
That his blood flows, or that his appetite
Is more to bread than stone; one who never feels
The wanton stings and motions of the sense,
But doth rebate and blunt his natural edge
With profits of the mind, study, and fast.
But he is a devil in private brawl, the most skilful,

Bloody and fatal opposite; souls and bodies
Hath he divorced three. Let me play the fool:
With mirth and laughter let old wrinkles come,
And let my liver rather heat with wine
Than my heart cool with mortifying groans.
Why should a man, whose blood is warm within,
Sit like his grandsire cut in alabaster?

Rinaldo. But hear thee, Perfumo;
Thou art too wild, too rude and bold of voice;
Parts that become thee happily enough
And in such eyes as ours appear not faults;
But where thou art not known, why, there they show
Something too liberal. Pray thee, take pain
To allay with some cold drops of modesty
Thy skipping spirit, lest through thy wild behavior
I be misconstrued in the place I go to.

Perfumo. Signior Rinaldo, hear me:
If I do not put on a sober habit,
Talk with respect and swear but now and then,
Wear prayer-books in my pocket, look demurely,
Use all the observance of civility,
Like one well studied in sad ostent
To please his grandam, never trust me more.

Rinaldo. Well, we shall see your bearing.

Perfumo. Nay, but I bar to-night: you shall not gauge me
By what we do to-night!
Mistress Closet! A quart of ale!

Blackout.

ACT I

Scene 4

Palermo. Garden of the royal palace. Enter Musik,
Camillo, and Morelli.

Camillo. We are sorry you must go. We love the Duke
Valmond, an absolute gentleman, full of most excellent
differences, of very soft society and great showing:
indeed, to speak feelingly of him, he is the card or
calendar of gentry, we find in him the continent of
what part a gentleman would see.

Morelli. He hears merry tales and smiles not: I fear he will
prove the weeping philosopher when he grows old,
being so full of unmannerly sadness in his youth.
Is he disposed to mirth?

Musik. He does confess he feels himself distracted;
There's something in his soul
O'er which his melancholy sits on brood.

Morelli. Yet seemeth he too melancholy,
As if the entertainment in our court
Had not a show might countervail his worth.

Musik. Weigh him well,
And that which looks like pride is courtesy.

Enter Amadeo, Sophia, Valmond, Katrina, Lucinda, and
Beauchance.

Valmond. Two months now since we have left our throne
Without a burthen: time as long again
Would be fill'd up, my brother, with our thanks;
And yet we should, for perpetuity,
Go hence in debt;
We take our leave with many thousand thanks.

Amadeo. Stay your thanks a while;
        And pay them when you part.

Valmond. Sir, that's tomorrow. My ships are ready and
        My people did expect my hence departure
        Two days ago.
        I am question'd by my fears, of what may chance
        Or breed upon our absence.

Sophia. One seven-night longer.

Valmond. Very soothe, tomorrow, Princess. My affairs
        Do even drag me homeward: which to hinder
        Were in your love a whip to me; my stay
        To you a charge and trouble: to save both,
        Farewell, our brother and noble hostess.

Amadeo. Ere thee depart, we'll share a bounteous time
        In different pleasures. Pray you, let us in.

        *Exit Amadeo, Sophia, Musik, Camillo, and Morelli
                severally.*

Beauchance. Shall we be sunder'd? shall we part, sweet
        girl?

Lucinda. Strangle such thoughts as these with any thing
        That you behold the while. I cannot be
        Mine own, nor any thing to any, if
        I be not thine.
        Sweet Count, will you be true?

Beauchance. Who I? Alas, it is my vice, my fault.
        For such as I am all true lovers are,
        Unstaid and skittish in all motions else,
        Save in the constant image of the creature
        That is beloved.
        Here is my hand for my true constancy;
        And when that hour o'erslips me in the day
        Wherein I sigh not, Lucinda, for thy sake,

The next ensuing hour some foul mischance
Torment me for my love's forgetfulness!

Lucinda. If you depart from me, I cannot live.
Were you but riding forth to air yourself,
Such parting were too petty. Look here, love,
This diamond was my grandam's: take it, heart.

Beauchance. (*Taking the diamond.*) Sweet Lucinda, for
my sake wear this;
It is a manacle of love; I'll place it
Upon this fairest prisoner.
(*Putting a bracelet upon her arm.*)

Lucinda. O the gods!
When shall we see each other again?

They embrace.

Beauchance. O, let me stay, befall what may befall!

Lucinda. Away! Let me hear from thee;
For wheresoe'er thou art in this world's globe
I'll have an Iris that shall find thee out.
Take my heart with thee.

Beauchance. Should we be taking leave
As long a term as yet we have to live,
The loathness to depart would grow.
Come, kiss; and let us part. Adieu!

Lucinda. So now farewell; and farewell life with thee!

Beauchance. No! Not yet! By heaven. Can you devise
Some means to come to shrift this evening?
For there we shall be shrived and married.

Lucinda. I can! I shall! Dearest Beauchance,
O'er my spirit thy full supremacy
Thou know'st, and that thy beck might from
The bidding of the Lord command me.

Exit Beauchance and *Lucinda.*

Valmond. Whether we shall meet again I know not.

Katrina. If not, why then, this parting was well made.

Valmond. Time bids be gone.

Katrina. Love, friendship, charity, are subjects all
        To envious and calumniating time.

Valmond. Yea. The time of life is short.
        To spend that shortness basely were too long.

Katrina. Then fair hope must hinder life's decay. Have
        you not heard that Time travels in divers paces with
        divers persons? I'll tell you who Time ambles withal,
        who Time trots withal, who Time gallops withal and
        who he stands still withal.

Valmond. I prithee, who doth he trot withal?

Katrina. Marry, he trots hard with a young maid between
        the contract of her marriage and the day it is
        solemnized: if the interim be but a se'nnight, Time's
        pace is so hard that it seems the length of seven year.

Valmond. Who ambles Time withal?

Katrina. With a priest that lacks Latin and sleeps easily
        because he cannot study, lacking the burden of lean
        and wasteful learning.

Valmond. Who doth he gallop withal?

Katrina. With a thief to the gallows, for though he go as
        softly as foot can fall, he thinks himself too soon there.

Valmond. Who stays it still withal?

Katrina. With lawyers in the vacation, for they sleep
between term and term and then they perceive not
how Time moves.
(*pause*)
I speak too long; but 'tis to peize the time,
To eke it and to draw it out in length,
Until our stars that frown lend us a smile.
What fates impose that we must needs abide.

Valmond. Still? Shall we curse the planets of mishap?

Katrina. But who can control his fate? 'tis not so now.

Valmond. Do you give me leave to speak my mind?

Katrina. Speak, sir. Let me know your mind;
Teach me how I should forget to think.

Valmond. It is the excellent foppery of the world, that,
when we are sick in fortune—often the surfeit of our
own behavior—we make guilty of our disasters the sun,
the moon, and the stars: as if we were fools by
heavenly compulsion, spherical predominance, an
enforced obedience of planetary influence, and a
divine thrusting on: an admirable evasion of man, to
lay his life to the charge of a star! The power and
corrigible authority of life lies in our wills.

Katrina. Who taught you this?

Valmond. Experience, Princess. Observation.
(*beat*)
I am too bold. I ask your pardon.

Katrina. My lord, there needs no such apology.
The weight of this sad time we must obey;
Speak what we feel, not what we ought to say.
(*Aside.*) Yet hold I off.
Though my heart's content firm love doth bear,
Nothing of that shall from mine eyes appear.

Valmond. (*Aside.*) As plays the sun upon the glassy
   streams,
  Twinkling another counterfeited beam,
  So seems this gorgeous beauty to mine eyes.
  Fain would I woo her, yet I dare not speak:
  Fie, hast not a tongue? is she not here?
  Ay, beauty's princely majesty is such,
  Confounds the tongue and makes the senses rough.

Katrina. (*Aside.*) O constancy, be strong upon my side,
  Set a huge mountain 'tween my heart and tongue!
  I have a man's mind, but a woman's might.
  How hard it is for women to keep counsel!
    (*To Valmond.*)
  Duke Valmond.

*Katrina removes chain from around her neck and gives it
to him.*

Katrina. (*Cont'd.*) Wear this for me. Remember my good
  will.

Valmond. (*Aside.*) Can I not say, I thank you?
  What passion hangs these weights upon my tongue?
  I cannot speak to her.
  Unhappy that I am, I cannot heave
  My heart into my mouth.

Valmond opens mouth as if to speak.

Katrina. Did you call, sir?

Valmond shakes his head.

Katrina. Fare you well.

Exit Katrina. Blackout.

ACT II

Scene 1

Palermo. Council chamber in the palace. Morelli.

Morelli. I do but dream on sovereignty;
    Like one that stands upon a promontory,
    And spies a far-off shore where he would tread,
    Wishing his foot were equal with his eye,
    And chides the sea that sunders him from thence,
    Saying, he'll lade it dry to have his way:
    So do I wish the crown, being so far off;
    And so I chide the means that keeps me from it
    And, since this earth affords no joy to me,
    But to command, to cheque, to o'erbear such
    As are of better person than myself,
    I'll make my heaven to dream upon the crown.
    I will be still awhile till time do serve:
    I'll watch and wake when others be asleep;
    When I spy advantage, I'll claim the crown,
    For that's the golden mark I seek to hit.

Enter Camillo.

Camillo. Good morrow, brother. Why, what's the matter,
    That you have such a February face,
    So full of frost, of storm and cloudiness?

Morelli. Men judge by the complexion of the sky
    The state and inclination of the day:
    So may you by my dull and heavy eye.

Enter in state King Lucentio, Amadeo, and Lords.

Morelli. God and his angels guard your sacred throne
    And make you long become it!

Lucentio. Sure, we thank you. Now we are well resolved;
　　Call in the messenger sent from Naples;
　　Tell their general we attend him here,
　　To know for what he comes, and whence he comes,
　　And what he craves.

　　　　　Exit Camillo.

Lucentio. (Cont'd.) I had a thing to say, but let it go;
　　I will fit it with some better time.
　　The sun is in the heaven.

　　　　Re-enter Camillo with Lord Tertius.

Camillo. My King; Lord Tertius,
　　Sent by Prince Cosimo, son of Naples.

Tertius. (Bowing.) May't please your majesty to give us
　　　　leave
　　Freely to render what we have in charge;
　　Or shall we sparingly show you far off
　　The Prince's meaning and our embassy?

Lucentio. With frank and with uncurbed plainness,
　　Tell us the Prince's mind.

Tertius. When King Pompeo was in this island
　　And conquer'd it, thy royal uncle, for him
　　And his succession granted Naples a tribute,
　　Yearly three thousand pounds, which by thee lately
　　Is left untender'd.

Amadeo. And, to kill the marvel, shall be so ever.
　　Sicily is a world by itself;
　　And we will nothing pay for wearing our own noses.

Tertius. We are come to this isle of Sicily
　　For the demand of our neglected tribute.

Lucentio. That opportunity
　　Which Naples had to take from 's, to resume
　　We have again.

Come, our kingdom is stronger than it was.
Why tribute? why should we pay tribute? If Naples
can hide the sun from us with a blanket, or put the
moon in his pocket, we will pay him tribute for light;
else, sir, no more tribute, pray you now.

Camillo. You must know, Lord Tertius,
     Till the Neapolitans did extort
     This tribute from us, we were free: your ambition
     Did put the yoke upon 's; which to shake off
     Becomes a warlike people, whom we reckon
     Ourselves to be.

Lords All. We do.

Lucentio. I am perfect that the Dalmatians for
     Their liberties are now in arms; a precedent
     Which not to read would show Sicilians cold:
     So the Neapolitans shall not find them.
     Say, then, there's no more tribute to be paid.
     Tell Prince Cosimo I will keep my state,
     Be like a king and show my sail of greatness.

Tertius. The hearts of princes kiss obedience,
     So much they love it; but to stubborn spirits
     They swell, and grow as terrible as storms.
     I am sorry, lords of Sicily,
     That I am to pronounce the King of Naples thine
         enemy:
     Receive it from me, then: war and confusion
     In Naples' name pronounce I 'gainst thee: look
     For fury not to be resisted. Thus defied,
     I thank thee for myself.

Lucentio. Thou art welcome, sir.
     I know your master's pleasure and he mine.
     Our countrymen
     Are men more order'd than when Pompeo
     Smiled at their lack of skill, but found their courage
     Worthy his frowning at: their discipline,
     Now mingled with their courages, will make known

To their approvers they are people such
That mend upon the world. So fare you well.

Exit Tertius.

Morelli. This was a merry message.

Camillo. Hear me, my liege:
For mine own part, I could be well content
To entertain the lag-end of my life
With quiet hours; for I do protest,
I have not sought the day of this dislike.
But this Cosimo is a pestilence
That does infect the land.
Now 'tis the spring, and weeds are shallow-rooted;
Suffer them now, and they'll o'ergrow the garden.
He's a rank weed, and we must root him out.

Morelli. Let's purge this choler without letting blood:
This we prescribe, though no physician;
Deep malice makes too deep incision;
Forget, forgive; conclude and be agreed.

Camillo. Arm, arm, my lord; thou never had more cause.
Cosimo hath gather'd head; and a power
Of high-resolved men, bent to the spoil,
Hither marches amain.

Morelli. Wherefore do you so ill translate yourself
Out of the speech of peace that bears such grace,
Into the harsh and boisterous tongue of war;
Turning your books to graves, your ink to blood,
Your pens to lances and your eager tongue
To a trumpet and a point of war?
(*Aside.*) My soul, yet I know not why, hates
        nothing more than he.
Some devil whisper curses in mine ear,
And prompt me, that my tongue may utter forth
The venomous malice of my swelling heart!

Camillo. Remember, my liege,
    The kings your ancestors, together with
    The natural bravery of your isle, which stands
    As Neptune's park, ribbed and paled in
    With rocks unscalable and roaring waters,
    With sands that will not bear your enemies' boats,
    But suck them up to the topmast.
    The peace of heaven is theirs that lift their swords
    In such a just war.

Lucentio. I embrace this fortune patiently,
    Since not to be avoided it falls on me.
    For us, we will consider of this further.

            Lucentio begins to exit.

Morelli. My king, Camillo gives you ill counsel:
    The Prince of Naples is to be feared;
    With hostile forces he'll o'erspread the land,
    And with the ostent of war will look so huge,
    Amazement shall drive courage from the state;
    Our men be vanquish'd ere they do resist,
    And subjects punish'd that ne'er thought offence.
    My liege, my lord, the Duke of Syracuse
    Has spoken like a traitor, and shall answer
    As traitors do.
    We charge you, that you have contrived to wind
    Yourself into a power tyrannical;
    For which you are a traitor to the people,
    Conspirant 'gainst this high-illustrious king.

Camillo. Traitor? How now, my brother Messina!
    You mistake me, sir.
    The purest spring is not so free from mud
    As I am clear from treason to my sovereign.

Morelli. Smooth runs the water where the brook is deep;
    And in his simple show he harbours treason.
    Ah, gracious lord, these days are dangerous:
    Virtue is choked with foul ambition
    And charity chased hence by rancour's hand;

Foul subornation is predominant
And equity exiled your highness' land.

Camillo. Brother, you do me shameful injury,
Falsely to draw me in these vile suspects.
Back do I toss those treasons to thy head.

Morelli. I do profess that for your highness' good I ever
labour'd
More than mine own; that am, have, and will be—
Though all the world should crack their duty to you,
And throw it from their soul—yet my duty,
As doth a rock against the chiding flood,
Should the approach of this wild river break,
Stands unshaken yours.

Lucentio. No more!
Good Lord, what madness rules in brainsick men,
When for so slight and frivolous a cause
Such factious emulations shall arise!
Messina and Camillo, good brothers,
Quiet yourselves, I pray, and be at peace.
Our kinsman Camillo is as innocent
From meaning treason to our royal person
As is the sucking lamb or harmless dove:
The Duke is virtuous, mild and too well given
To dream on evil or to work my downfall.

Exit Lucentio and Amadeo one way, Morelli another.

Camillo. What louring star now envies my estate,
That my brother, the Duke of Messina,
Does seek subversion of my harmless life?
That never didst him wrong, nor no man wrong.

Exit Camillo.

First Lord. Who's so gross,
That seeth not this palpable device?

Second Lord. No simple man that sees
  This jarring discord of nobility,
  This shouldering of each other in the court,
  But that it doth presage some ill event.

First Lord. I will not trust the Duke of Messina;
  I do not like him; I know his spirit,
  And will not trust one of his malice.

Second Lord. Such men as he be never at heart's ease
  Whiles they behold a greater than themselves,
  And therefore are they very dangerous.

First Lord. 'Tis much when envy breeds unkind division;
  There comes the rain, there begins confusion.

Second Lord. Bad is the world; and all will come to
    nought,
  When such bad dealings must be seen in thought.

      Exit All. Blackout.

ACT II

Scene 2

Palermo. A room in the palace. Lucinda, Katrina, and Sophia.

Lucinda. O Katrina! O Sophia! that thou didst know how many fathom deep I am in love! But it cannot be sounded: my affection hath an unknown bottom, like the bay of Portugal.

Katrina. Be moderate; allay thy ecstasy.

Lucinda. I am undone; there is no living, none,
If Beauchance be away.

Katrina. Scant this excess.
(*Aside.*) If to do were as easy as to know what were good to do, chapels had been churches and poor men's cottages princes' palaces. It is a good divine that follows his own instructions: I can easier teach twenty what were good to be done, than be one of the twenty to follow mine own teaching.

Lucinda. O, know'st thou not his looks are my soul's food?
Pity the dearth that I have pined in,
By longing for that food so long a time.
Didst thou but know the inly touch of love,
Thou wouldst as soon go kindle fire with snow
As seek to quench the fire of love with words.

Katrina. I do not seek to quench your love's hot fire,
But qualify the fire's extreme rage,
Lest it should burn above the bounds of reason.

Lucinda. If ever—as that ever may be near—
You meet in some fresh cheek the power of fancy,
Then shall you know the wounds invisible

> That love's keen arrows make.
> Counsel, Sophia; gentle girl, assist me;
> And even in kind love I do conjure thee,
> To lesson me.

Sophia. If he says he loves you,
> It fits your wisdom so far to believe it
> As he may give his saying deed.
> Then weigh what loss your honour may sustain,
> If with too credent ear you list his songs,
> Or lose your heart, or your chaste treasure open
> To his unmaster'd importunity.
> And keep you in the rear of your affection,
> Out of the shot and danger of desire.
> The chariest maid is prodigal enough,
> If she unmask her beauty to the moon:
> Virtue itself 'scapes not calumnious strokes.

Lucinda. They do not love that do not show their love.

Sophia. O, they love least that let men know their love.

Katrina. (*Aside.*) And yet, good faith, I wish'd myself a
> man,
> Or that we women had men's privilege
> Of speaking first.

Lucinda. I did not take my leave of him, but had
> Most pretty things to say: ere I could tell him
> How I would think on him at certain hours
> Such thoughts and such, or I could make him swear
> The shes of Burgundy should not betray
> Mine interest and his honour, or have charged him,
> At the sixth hour of morn, at noon, at midnight,
> To encounter me with orisons, for then
> I am in heaven for him; or ere I could
> Give him that parting kiss which I had set
> Betwixt two charming words, comes in my father
> And like the tyrannous breathing of the north
> Shakes all our buds from growing.

Sophia. Sweet Lucinda, be merry. From henceforth, let us
    devise sports. What shall be our sport, then?

Lucinda. Since I am punish'd with my thwarting stars,
    Let us sit and mock the good housewife Fortune.

Katrina. But your better stars brought Beauchance to you.

Sophia. I thank my stars. I do believe it is the stars,
    The stars above that govern our conditions.

Katrina. I can no longer live by thinking thus.
    We have reason to cool our raging motions,
    Our carnal stings, and our unbitted lusts:
    'Tis in ourselves that we are thus or thus.

Lucinda. Where's the soothsayer that you praised so?

Sophia. Come, let's seek him out.

Katrina. I beg your pardons, ladies. Excuse me.
    (*Aside.*) I will persevere in my course of loyalty.

               Exit Sophia and Lucinda.

Katrina. I have done penance for contemning Love,
    Whose high imperious thoughts have punish'd me
    With bitter fasts, with penitential groans,
    With nightly tears and daily heart-sore sighs;
    For in revenge of my contempt of love,
    Love hath chased sleep from my enthralled eyes
    And made them watchers of mine own heart's sorrow.
    I, forsooth, in love! I, that have been love's whip;
    A very beadle to a humorous sigh;
    A critic, nay, a night-watch constable;
    A domineering pedant o'er the boy.
    O my little heart—
    And I to be a corporal of his field,
    And wear his colours like a tumbler's hoop!
    What, I! I love! O how strange it seems
    Not to believe, and yet too credulous!
    Thy weal and woe are both of them extremes;

Despair and hope makes thee ridiculous:
The one doth flatter thee in thoughts unlikely,
In likely thoughts the other kills thee quickly.
O gentle Valmond, Love's a mighty lord,
And hath so humbled me, as, I confess,
There is no woe to his correction,
Nor to his service no such joy on earth.
I know I love in vain, strive against hope:
Yet in this captious and intenible sieve
I still pour in the waters of my love.

Enter Amadeo.

Amadeo. Pardon me, sister. She's not here I seek for.
You sit patiently and inly ruminate.
What's the matter?

Katrina. Fate. Fortune. Time. Nothing.
What news from the Duke of Burgundy?

Amadeo. Prithee, speak to me as to thy thinkings.
It is said thou dost affect the duke.

Katrina. To you alone, Amadeo, I confess:
Under love's heavy burden do I sink.

Amadeo. But what's the matter?

Katrina. I do not know if he will return again.

Amadeo. If you affect him, sister, here I swear
I'll plead for you myself but you shall have him.
A man of sovereign parts he is esteem'd;
Well fitted in arts, glorious in arms:
Nothing becomes him ill that he would well.
I know him as myself; for from our infancy
We have conversed and spent our hours together:
And, in a word, for far behind his worth
Comes all the praises that I now bestow,
He is complete in feature and in mind

With all good grace to grace a gentleman.
Pray, let us go. I seek my wife.

Exit. Blackout.

ACT II

Scene 3

Burgundy. Park of Valmond's castle. Valmond.

Valmond. Why should this change of thoughts,
    The sad companion, dull-eyed melancholy,
    Be my so used a guest as not an hour,
    In the day's glorious walk, or peaceful night,
    The tomb where grief should sleep, can breed me
        quiet?
    Here pleasures court mine eyes, and mine eyes shun
        them,
    Yet neither pleasure's art can joy my spirits,
    Nor yet the other's distance comfort me.
    O melancholy!
    Who ever yet could sound thy bottom? find
    The ooze, to show what coast thy sluggish crare
    Might easiliest harbour in?

*Enter Beauchance from opposite direction, reading a
letter, unaware of Valmond.*

Beauchance. Sweet love! sweet lines! sweet life!
    Here is her hand, the agent of her heart;
    Here is her oath for love, her honour's pawn.
    O, that her father would applaud our loves,
    To seal our happiness with his consent!
    O heavenly Lucinda!

Beauchance sits down and takes out pen and paper.

Beauchance. (*Cont'd.*) Assist me, some extemporal god of
    rhyme, for I am sure I shall turn sonnet. Devise, wit;
    write, pen, as much love in rhyme as would be
    cramm'd up in a sheet of paper, for I am for whole
    volumes in folio. Marry, I cannot show it in rhyme, I

have tried: No, I was not born under a rhyming
planet.

*Valmond approaches, and Beauchance puts letter and
paper away.*

Valmond. What's the matter, my lord?

Beauchance. Between who?

Valmond. I mean, the matter that you read.
Was not that letter from fair Lucinda?

Beauchance. Dear friend, I must needs tell thee all.
By your gracious patience,
I would a round unvarnish'd tale deliver
Of my whole course of love and marriage.

Valmond. Your marriage!? Is't possible that on so little
acquaintance you should like her? that but seeing you
should love her? and loving woo? and, wooing, she
should grant?

Beauchance. Neither call the giddiness of it in question, the
small acquaintance, my sudden wooing, nor her sudden
consenting. Love's reason's without reason.

Valmond. Let me ask thee, Beauchance:
How shall I know if I am in love?

Beauchance. There are certain signs to know. An old
religious uncle of mine taught me how to know a man
in love.

Valmond. What were his marks?

Beauchance. A lean cheek, which you have not, a blue eye
and sunken, which you have not, an unquestionable
spirit, which you have not, a beard neglected, which
you have not; then your hose should be ungartered,
your sleeve unbuttoned, your shoe untied and every

thing about you demonstrating a careless desolation;
but you are no such man.

Valmond. Yet, my dear Count, I think I am in love.

Beauchance. Hast ever sigh'd upon a midnight pillow?
Hast ever been drawn by thy fantasy
To many actions most ridiculous?
If thou remember'st not the slightest folly
That ever love did make thee run into,
Thou hast not loved:
Or if thou hast not sat as I do,
Wearying thy hearer in thy mistress' praise,
Thou hast not loved:
Or if thou hast not broke from company
Abruptly, as my passion now makes me,
Thou hast not loved.
You are rather point-device in your accoutrements as
loving yourself than seeming the lover of any other.

Valmond. Yet there is a gentle lady;
When tongues speak sweetly, then they name her
name.

Beauchance. The fair Katrina.

Valmond. Beshrew me but I love her heartily;
For she is wise, if I can judge of her,
And fair she is, if that mine eyes be true,
And true she is, as she hath proved herself,
And therefore, like herself, wise, fair and true,
Shall she be placed in my constant soul.
In mine eye she is the sweetest lady that ever
I looked on.

Beauchance. Very sweet.
But if you love her, you cannot see her.

Valmond. Why?

Beauchance. Because love is blind and lovers cannot see.

Valmond. I do protest I never loved myself
    Till now infixed I beheld myself
    Drawn in the flattering table of her eye.
    Strike me, sir;
    Give me a gash, put me to present pain;
    Lest this great sea of joys rushing upon me
    O'erbear the shores of my mortality,
    And drown me with their sweetness.

Beauchance. O powerful love! that, in some respects,
    makes a beast a man, in some other, a man a beast.
    Now, sir, I shall tell you a pretty tale.

Exit.

ACT II

Scene 4

Palermo. Tavern. Perfumo, Rinaldo, Soldiers, after much drinking, and Boy.

Perfumo. What ho! Mistress Closet!
Another flagon of Rhenish, if you please.

Mistress Closet. (*Within.*) Anon!

Perfumo. Or a pot of ale, Signior Rinaldo?

Rinaldo. If there be money in thy purse.

Perfumo. (*Feels in his pockets and purse.*) Upon my life, I
fell asleep here and had my pocket picked. I have been
cozened. Thou fat, devilish knave.

Rinaldo. Signior Perfumo, you owe me money, and now
you pick a quarrel to beguile me of it! Thou art a
knave very voluble; no further conscionable than in
putting on the mere form of civil and humane
seeming; a subtle knave, a finder of occasions, that has
an eye can stamp and counterfeit advantages.

Perfumo. Ye fat paunch. Thou leathern-jerkin, crystal
button, agate-ring, puke-stocking, caddis-garter,
smooth-tongue—

Rinaldo. Thou art an arrant counterfeit rascal; a rogue,
that now and then goes to the wars, to grace himself at
his return under the form of a soldier.

Perfumo. I know thee a notorious liar, and solely a
coward.
Out, alas, sir! Cozenage, mere cozenage.

Rinaldo. Thou art a villain to impeach me thus:
I'll prove mine honour and mine honesty
Against thee presently, if thou darest stand.

Perfumo. I do defy you, and spit at you;
Win me and wear me; let him answer me.
Come, follow me, boy; come, sir boy, come, follow me:
Sir boy, I'll whip you from your foining fence;
I know thee, yea, even to the utmost scruple—
Scambling, out-facing, fashion-monging boys,
That speak off half a dozen dangerous words,
How they may hurt their enemies, if they durst;
And this is all.

Rinaldo. There's neither honesty, manhood, nor good
fellowship in thee.

Perfumo. How now, wool sack!

Perfumo draws his sword. Rinaldo draws his.

Perfumo. (*Cont'd.*) You whoreson round man! Ye fat-
kidneyed rascal!

Rinaldo. You starveling, you elf-skin! You scullion! You
Rampallion! You fustian rascal!

Perfumo. Thou trunk of humours, huge hill of flesh!

Rinaldo. Beggarly, three-suited, hundred-pound, worsted-
stocking knave!

Perfumo. Huge bombard of sack, stuffed cloak-bag of
guts!

Rinaldo. You dried neat's tongue, you bull's pizzle!

Perfumo. Thou clay-brained guts, thou crusty batch of
nature!

Rinaldo. You cut-purse rascal! filthy bung! bottle-ale
rascal!

Perfumo. Thou globe of sinful continents! Thou full dish of fool! Thou whoreson, obscene, grease-tallow catch, bed-presser. Horseback-breaker!

Rinaldo. You ruinous butt! You whoreson indistinguishable cur! Idle immaterial skein of sleave-silk! Lily-livered, glass-gazing, super-serviceable finical rogue.

Perfumo. Thou impudent, embossed toadstool! Thou beef-witted, sodden-witted cobloaf! One whom I will beat into clamorous whining, if thou deniest the least syllable of thy addition!

Rinaldo. Thou thing of no bowels, thou!

Perfumo. You bolting-hutch of beastliness, swollen parcel of dropsies!

Rinaldo. Thou art a hungry lean-faced villain,
A mere anatomy, a mountebank,
A needy, hollow-eyed, cogging, cozening knave!

Perfumo. Scurvy slave!

Rinaldo. Varlet!

Perfumo. Wretch!

Rinaldo. Bawd!

Perfumo. Thief!

Enter Mistress Closet.

Mistress Closet. My masters, are you mad! Or what are you? Have ye no wit, manners? Is there no respect of place, persons, nor time in you? I'll no swaggerers: I am in good name and fame. I have not lived all this while, to have swaggering now! By my troth, this is the old fashion; you two never meet but you fall to some

discord: you are both, i' good truth, as rheumatic as
two dry toasts; you cannot one bear with another's
confirmities.

Soldier. For my part I say the gentlemen have drunk
themselves out of their five sentences.

Perfumo. I'll ne'er be drunk whilst I live again, but in
honest, civil, godly company, for this trick: if I be
drunk, I'll be drunk with those that have the fear of
God, and not with drunken knaves.

Rinaldo. I cannot remember what I did when you made
me drunk. O God, that men should put an enemy in
their mouths to steal away their brains! that we
should transform ourselves into beasts!

Mistress Closet. Be friends, for shame, be friends.

Perfumo. Let me have thy hand: and from this hour
The heart of brothers govern in our loves.
Mistress Closet, that bottle of sack, if you please.

Exit Mistress Closet. Perfumo looks over Rinaldo's dress.

Perfumo. In companions
That do converse and waste the time together,
Whose souls do bear an equal yoke of love,
There must needs be a like proportion
Of lineaments, of manners and of spirit.
I do think thee to be a pretty wise fellow; yet the scarfs
and the bannerets about thee do manifoldly dissuade
me from believing thee a vessel of too great burthen.

Soldier. The soul of this man is his clothes.

Rinaldo. But I am a courtier. Seest thou not the air of the
court in these enfoldings? hath not my gait in it the
measure of the court? receives not thy nose court-odor
from me? I am courtier cap-a-pe.

Perfumo. O, no doubt, thou hast trod a measure, flattered a lady, undone three tailors, had four quarrels, and like to have fought one. All this I see; and I see that the fashion wears out more apparel than the man. Seest thou not, I say, what a deformed thief this fashion is? how giddily a' turns about all the hot bloods between fourteen and five-and-thirty? Will you win your love in yellow stockings?

Rinaldo. Why, how know you that I am in love?

Perfumo. Marry, by these special marks: first, you have learned to wreathe your arms, like a malecontent; to relish a love-song, like a robin-redbreast; to sigh, like a school-boy that had lost his A B C; to weep, like a young wench that had buried her grandam; to fast, like one that takes diet; to watch like one that fears robbing; to speak puling, like a beggar at Hallowmas. You were wont, when you laughed, to crow like a cock; when you walked, to walk like one of the lions; when you fasted, it was presently after dinner; when you looked sadly, it was for want of money: and now you are metamorphosed with a mistress.

Rinaldo. Are all these things perceived in me?

Perfumo. These follies are within you and shine through you like the water in an urinal, that not an eye that sees you but is a physician to comment on your malady.

Rinaldo. Can you advise me?

Perfumo. First, let thy love be younger than thyself,
Or thy affection cannot hold the bent;
For women are as roses, whose fair flower
Being once display'd, doth fall that very hour.
Tell me thy reason why thou wilt marry.

Rinaldo. My poor body requires it: I am driven on by the flesh, and he must needs go that the devil drives.

Perfumo. Use her at thy pleasure: crack the glass of her
    virginity, and make the rest malleable.

Rinaldo. She doth barricado with warlike resistance.

Perfumo. Then lay an amiable siege to her honesty: use
    your art of wooing; win her to consent to you.

Rinaldo. She will not stay the siege of loving terms,
    Nor bide the encounter of asserting eyes.

Perfumo. Take her hearing prisoner with the force
    And strong encounter of thy amorous tale.
    Tell her plain,
    She sings as sweetly as a nightingale:
    Say she looks as clear
    As morning roses newly wash'd with dew:
    Commend her volubility,
    And say she uttereth piercing eloquence:
    If she do bid you pack, give her thanks,
    As though she bid you stay by her a week:
    If she deny to wed, then crave the day
    When you shall ask the banns and when be married.
    Win her with gifts, if she respect not words:
    Dumb jewels often in their silent kind
    More than quick words do move a woman's mind.

Rinaldo. But she did scorn a present that I sent her.
    She will not ope her lap to saint-seducing gold.

Perfumo. A woman sometimes scorns what best contents
      her.
    Send her another; never give her o'er;
    For scorn at first makes after-love the more.
    If she do frown, 'tis not in hate of you,
    But rather to beget more love in you:
    If she do chide, 'tis not to have you gone;
    For why, the fools are mad, if left alone.
    Take no repulse, whatever she doth say;
    For "get you gone," she doth not mean "away!"
    Flatter and praise, commend, extol their graces;

Though ne'er so black, say they have angels' faces.
That man that hath a tongue, I say, is no man,
If with his tongue he cannot win a woman.

Rinaldo. I cannot. Methinks sometimes I have no more
    wit than a Christian or an ordinary man has: but I am
    a great eater of beef and I believe that does harm to
    my wit.

Perfumo. Tut, tut. Say to her:
    "I would outstare the sternest eyes that look,
    Outbrave the heart most daring on the earth,
    Pluck the young sucking cubs from the she-bear,
    Yea, mock the lion when he roars for prey,
    To win thee, lady."

Rinaldo. She hath forsworn to love, and in that vow
    Do I live dead that live to tell it now.

            Enter Mistress Closet with bottle of sack.

Perfumo. Give me some music; music, moody food of
    Us that trade in love.

Rinaldo. I love a ballad but even too well, if it be doleful
    matter merrily set down, or a very pleasant thing
    indeed and sung lamentably.

Perfumo. Sing, boy, my spirit grows heavy in love.

Boy. (*Sings.*)
            Tell me where is fancy bred
            Or in the heart, or in the head?
            How begot, how nourished?
            Reply, reply,
            It is engender'd in the eyes
            With gazing fed; and fancy dies
            In the cradle where it lies.
            Let us all ring fancy's knell
            I'll begin it,—Ding, dong, bell.

Perfumo. And is not my hostess of the tavern a most sweet
      wench?
    Now, by the world, she is a lusty wench;
    I love her ten times more than e'er I did.
    O, how I long to have some chat with her!

Mistress Closet. Hie you home to bed.
    Thou subtle, perjured, false, disloyal man!

Perfumo. To what, my love, shall I compare thine eyne?
    Crystal is muddy. O, how ripe in show
    Thy lips, those kissing cherries, tempting grow!
    When thou hold'st up thy hand: O, let me kiss
    This princess of pure white, this seal of bliss!

Mistress Closet. You whoreson chops.
    Think'st thou I am so shallow, so conceitless
    To be seduced by thy flattery,
    That hast deceived so many with thy vows?

Perfumo. Sit on my knee, dear.

Mistress Closet. Thou little whoreson pint-pot, when wilt
    thou leave fighting o' days and foining o' nights, and
    begin to patch up thine old body for heaven?

Perfumo. Peace, do not speak like a death's-head; do not
    bid me remember mine end. I am old, I am old.

Mistress Closet. I love thee better than I love e'er a scurvy
    young boy of them all.

Perfumo. Thou'lt forget me when I am gone.

Mistress Closet. By my troth, thou'lt set me a-weeping, an
    thou sayest so.

Perfumo. Think what a man is; consider his frailty. Think
    of that.

Soldier. Is it not strange that desire should so many years
    outlive performance?

Enter Second Soldier in a rush.

Perfumo. How now! What's the matter?

Second Soldier. I tell you what: war!
    We must away to court, signiors, presently;
    A dozen captains stay at door for us.

Perfumo. Farewell, hostess; farewell. You see how men of
    merit are sought after: the undeserver may sleep, when
    the man of action is called on. Farewell. Rinaldo, pay
    the musicians. Gentlemen, we must all to the wars.

Exit All.

ACT II

Scene 5

Palermo. A room in the palace. Amadeo, Adrianna,
Sophia, and Katrina.

Amadeo. Farewell, my dearest sister, fare thee well:
  The elements be kind to thee, and make
  Thy spirits all of comfort! fare thee well.
  Mother, come, leave your tears: a brief farewell.
  Nay, mother,
  Where is your ancient courage? you were used
  To say extremity was the trier of spirits;
  That common chances common men could bear;
  That when the sea was calm all boats alike
  Show'd mastership in floating.
  You were used to load me
  With precepts that would make invincible
  The heart that conn'd them.

Adrianna. Amadeo, the middle of humanity thou never
  Knewest, but the extremity at both ends.
  Be advised: direct
  Yourself with the sap of reason and quench,
  Or but allay, the fire of passion.
  Moreover, be able for thine enemy
  Rather in power than use, and keep thy friend
  Under thy own life's key. What heaven more will,
  That thee may furnish and my prayers pluck down,
  Fall on thy head!

Amadeo. Madam, I desire your holy wishes. Pray to God.
  Dearest Sophia! What say'st thou, my lady?

Sophia. And must we be divided? Must we part?

Amadeo. Ay, hand from hand, my love, not heart from
  heart.

Sophia. In thy faint slumbers I by thee have watch'd,
    And heard thee murmur tales of iron wars;
    Thy spirit within thee hath been so at war
    And thus hath so bestirr'd thee in thy sleep,
    That beads of sweat have stood upon thy brow
    Like bubbles in a late-disturbed stream;
    And in thy face strange motions have appear'd,
    Such as we see when men restrain their breath
    On some great sudden hest. O, what portents are
        these?
    Methinks,
    Some unborn sorrow, ripe in fortune's womb,
    Is coming towards me, and my inward soul
    With nothing trembles: at some thing it grieves.
    Come, I will fasten on this sleeve of thine.
    As thou lovest thy life—

Amadeo. Most dearest wife,
    Life every man holds dear; but the brave man
    Holds honour far more precious-dear than life.
    The strong necessity of time commands
    Our services; but my full heart
    Remains in use with you.

       Amadeo tries to kiss Sophia. She holds him off.

Sophia. Pray you, seek no colour for your going,
    But bid farewell, and go.

Amadeo. Dearest chuck—

Sophia. O yet, for God's sake, go not to these wars!
    O, be persuaded!

Amadeo. Come, dearest madam. O, no tears, no tears.
    We make woe wanton with this fond delay:
    Come, come, in wooing sorrow let's be brief;
    One kiss shall stop our mouths, and dumbly part.

          They embrace and kiss.

Amadeo. (*Cont'd.*) Thus give I mine, and thus take I thy
    heart.

Sophia. Give me mine own again; 'twere no good part
    To take on me to keep and kill thy heart.

They kiss again.

Sophia. So, now I have mine own again, be gone,
    That I might strive to kill it with a groan.

Amadeo. Once more, adieu; the rest let sorrow say.

Exit Amadeo.

Sophia. Before God, my knee shall bow my prayers.
    O you leaden messengers,
    That ride upon the violent speed of fire,
    Fly with false aim; move the still-peering air,
    That sings with piercing; do not touch my lord.

Blackout.

ACT II

Scene 6

*Sicily. Before tent of Lucentio in a field outside Palermo.
Camillo, Amadeo, Morelli, Lords, and Captains.*

First Lord. How bloodily the sun begins to peer
    Above yon busky hill! the day looks pale
    At his distemperature.

Amadeo. I hear the king my father is sore sick.

Camillo. So 'tis reported, sir.

        Lucentio emerges from his tent.

Amadeo. How fares your majesty?

Lucentio. Health, alack, with youthful wings is flown
    From this bare wither'd trunk.
    This fever, that hath troubled me so long,
    Lies heavy on me. How goes the day?

First Captain. So please your majesty,
    Cosimo's legions, all from Napoli drawn,
    Are landed on your coast.

Lucentio. What a tide of woes
    Comes rushing on this woeful land at once!
    I know not what to do.

Camillo. Good my liege,
    Your preparation can affront no less
    Than what you hear of: come more, for more you're
      ready:
    The want is but to put those powers in motion
    That long to move.

Let's meet the time as it seeks us. We fear
Not what can from Napoli annoy us.

Lucentio. No doubt, if each man do his best.

Amadeo. I doubt not that; since we are well persuaded
We carry not a heart with us
That grows not in a fair consent with ours.

Lucentio. Then pause not; for the present time's so sick,
That present medicine must be minister'd,
Defend the justice of our cause with arms,
And, countrymen, my loving followers,
Plead my title with your swords.

First Lord. Never was monarch better fear'd and loved
Than is your majesty.

Camillo. Will you sit down, my liege?

Attendant brings stool for Lucentio. He sits.

Lucentio. More than we have said, loving countrymen,
The leisure and enforcement of the time
Forbids to dwell upon: yet remember this,
God and our good cause fight upon our side.
You, worthy brother, Duke of Syracuse,
Shall, with my son, noble Amadeo,
Lead our first battle.

Amadeo. The time and my intents are savage-wild,
More fierce and more inexorable far
Than empty tigers or the roaring sea!

Lucentio. Prince, I beseech you, hear me:
Heat not a furnace for your foe so hot
That it do singe yourself: we may outrun,
By violent swiftness, that which we run at,
And lose by over-running. Know you not,
The fire that mounts the liquor till't run o'er,
In seeming to augment it wastes it?

You must needs learn to amend this fault:
Though sometimes it show greatness, courage, blood.

Amadeo. Father, I am school'd.
I humbly do beseech you of your pardon.

Morelli. (*Aside.*) I will work him
To an exploit, now ripe in my device,
Under the which he shall not choose but fall:
And for his death no wind of blame shall breathe,
But even his mother shall uncharge the practise
And call it accident.

Camillo. We must attend his majesty's command.

Amadeo. The future comes apace.
O God! that one might read the book of fate,
And see the revolution of the times
Make mountains level, and the continent,
Weary of solid firmness, melt itself
Into the sea! and, other times, to see
The beachy girdle of the ocean
Too wide for Neptune's hips; how chances mock,
And changes fill the cup of alteration
With divers liquors!

Camillo. If this were seen,
The happiest youth, viewing his progress through,
What perils past, what crosses to ensue,
Would shut the book, and sit him down and die.

Lucentio. I am weary.
For this time I will leave you.

Amadeo and Camillo assist Lucentio into the tent.

First Lord. Princes have but their tides for their glories,
An outward honour for an inward toil;
Uneasy lies the head that wears a crown.

Second Lord. Who alone suffers suffers most i' the mind,
    But when grief hath mates, and bearing fellowship,
    How light and portable the pain seems.

Amadeo emerges from tent.

Amadeo. See how the morning opes her golden gates,
    And takes farewell of the glorious sun!
    How well resembles it the prime of youth,
    Trimm'd like a younker prancing to his love.
    Come on, brave soldiers; doubt not of the day.
    Our doubts are traitors,
    And make us lose the good we oft might win
    By fearing to attempt.
    If we are mark'd to die, we are enow
    To do our country loss; and if to live,
    The fewer men, the greater share of honour.
    Let each man do his best: and here draw I
    A sword, whose temper I intend to stain
    With the best blood that I can meet withal
    In the adventure of this perilous day.
    By heaven, methinks it were an easy leap,
    To pluck bright honour from the pale-faced moon,
    Or dive into the bottom of the deep,
    Where fathom-line could never touch the ground,
    And pluck up drowned honour by the locks;
    So he that doth redeem her thence might wear
    Without corrival, all her dignities.
    Sound all the lofty instruments of war,
    And by that music let us all embrace.
    Advance your standards, draw your willing swords.
    If we no more meet till we meet in heaven,
    Then, joyfully, adieu.

All. To arms!

Exit All.

ACT II

Scene 7

A plain outside Palermo. Alarums. Excursions. Enter Morelli and small force, then exit in retreat, followed by Cosimo and his forces. Enter Amadeo, leading Sicilians and driving Cosimo and his forces out.

Amadeo. A plague upon that sluggard Morelli,
    That thus delays my promised supply.
    Duke Camillo doth expect my aid,
    And I am lowted by a hapless villain.

Alarums. Re-enter Cosimo, Tertius, and forces, driving out Amadeo and Sicilians.

Cosimo. Sicilians, hear Cosimo of Naples:
    Unthread the rude eye of rebellion,
    And welcome home again your masters.

Morelli brought in as prisoner.

Morelli. Worthy Prince, on my knees I beg of you:
    Make my misery serve thy turn: so use it
    That my revengeful services may prove
    As benefits to thee, for I will fight
    Against my canker'd country with the spleen
    Of all the under fiends.

Cosimo. I know thy quality. What is thy name?

Morelli. Morelli, Duke of Messina. I will follow thee
    To the last gasp, with truth and loyalty.
    Here is my hand;
    Thy will by my performance shall be served.

Cosimo. And thy conscience?

Morelli. Ay, sir; where lies that? if 'twere a kibe,
  'Twould put me to my slipper: but I feel not
  This deity in my bosom.

Cosimo. And thy allegiance to Sicily?

Morelli. To hell, allegiance! vows, to the blackest devil!
  Conscience and grace, to the profoundest pit!
  I dare damnation.

Cosimo. How wilt thou serve me?

Morelli. I have a trick, a snare to trap your enemy.

Cosimo. Lead him forth.

    Soldiers lead out Morelli.

Tertius. The duke is a man full of deep deceit.

Cosimo. Treason is but trusted like the fox
  Who, ne'er so tame, so cherish'd and lock'd up,
  Will have a wild trick of his ancestors.
  He may yet serve our turn, or be ransomed.

 *Alarums. Exit Cosimo and his forces. Enter Amadeo and
     First Captain.*

First Captain. The time is troublesome, Prince.

Amadeo. Brief, then; what's the news?

First Captain. O, my sweet sir, news
  Black, fearful, comfortless and horrible.

Amadeo. Show me the very wound of this ill news:
  I am no woman, I'll not swoon at it.

First Captain. Fly you must; uncurable discomfit
  Reigns in the hearts of all our present parts.
  Away, for your relief! and we will live
  To see their day and them our fortune give.

Amadeo. Never! Not I.

First Captain. I think our country sinks beneath the yoke;
     It weeps, it bleeds, and each new hour a gash
     Is added to her wounds.

Amadeo. Then let the earth be drunken with our blood:
     I will not fly.
     Why stand we like soft-hearted women here,
     Wailing our losses, whiles the foe doth rage;
     And look upon, as if the tragedy
     Were play'd in jest by counterfeiting actors?
     We will not from the helm to set and weep.
     Here on my knee I vow to God above,
     I'll never pause again, never stand still.

First Captain. Now bid me run,
     And with a heart new-fired I follow you;
     And I will strive with things impossible;
     Yea, get the better of them. What's to do?

Amadeo. Follow me, then.

     Exit Amadeo and First Captain. Alarums. Excursions.
           Enter Camillo and his forces.

Camillo. In the midst of this bright-shining day,
     I spy a black, suspicious, threatening cloud,
     That will encounter with our glorious sun,
     Ere he attain his easeful western bed.

           Enter Tertius and his forces.

Tertius. The day is ours, noble Sicilian;
     The Prince of Naples doth rule in this realm;
     Pay him tribute, and submit thyself;
     Withdraw you and abate your strength;
     Dismiss your followers and, as suitors should,
     Plead your deserts in peace and humbleness.
     If you frown upon this proffer'd peace,
     You tempt the fury of my three attendants,

Lean famine, quartering steel, and climbing fire.
Who in a moment even with the earth
Shall lay your stately and air-braving towers,
If you forsake the offer of their love.

Camillo. I cannot nor I will not yield to you.
Ere the glass, that now begins to run,
Finish the process of his sandy hour,
These eyes, that see thee now well coloured,
Shall see thee wither'd, bloody, pale and dead.

Drums afar off.

Camillo. (*Cont'd.*) Alas, poor country!
Almost afraid to know itself.

*Alarums. Exit Camillo and forces in retreat, followed out
by Tertius and forces. Excursions. Enter Amadeo.*

Amadeo. The army of Naples hath got the field.

Enter Morelli.

Amadeo. Who goes there?

Morelli. A friend. Thy uncle, Duke of Messina.

Amadeo. What's the matter? Where are thy followers?

Morelli beckons Amadeo to follow him.

Morelli. We are too open here to argue this.
Let us seek out some desolate shade, and there
Weep our sad bosoms empty.

Amadeo. Let us rather
Hold fast the mortal sword, and like good men
Bestride our down-fall'n birthdom.
The powers of us may serve so great a day,
Come, let us take a muster speedily.

*Cosimo and Tertius emerge from an ambush, swords
drawn. They surround Amadeo.*

Amadeo. False traitor! Slave! Villainous contriver against
the king, your natural brother.

Cosimo. Lay down your weapons, Prince of Sicily.
The battle's lost. Surrender.

Amadeo. The hour is come to end the one of us.

*They fight. Morelli from behind wounds Amadeo. Cosimo
stabs Amadeo. He falls.*

Amadeo. O Sicily, I fear thy overthrow
More than my body's parting with my soul!
Bootless are plaints, and cureless are my wounds;
These eyes, like lamps whose wasting oil is spent,
Wax dim, as drawing to their exigent;
These feet, whose strengthless stay is numb, are
Unable to support this lump of clay,
Swift-winged with desire to get a grave,
As witting I no other comfort have.
My life is run its compass.
And now the arbitrator of despairs,
Just death, kind umpire of men's miseries,
With sweet enlargement doth dismiss me hence.
Here burns my candle out; ay, here it dies.

Amadeo dies.

Cosimo. Thus ever did rebellion find rebuke.
Adieu; ignominy sleep with thee in the grave,
But not remember'd in thy epitaph!
This is a conquest for a prince to boast of.
Prepare to enter the city.
We must proceed as we do find the people.

Morelli. Most noble sir, if you do hold the same intent
herein you wish'd us parties, we'll deliver you of any
danger.

Cosimo. Go tell the lords o' Palermo, I am here:
          Deliver them this paper: having read it,
          Bid them repair to the market place; where I,
          Even in theirs and in the commons' ears,
          Will vouch the truth of it.

Morelli. I'll acquaint our duteous citizens
          With all your just proceedings in this cause.
              (*Aside, departing with paper.*)
          In following him, I follow but myself;
          Heaven is my judge, not I for love and duty,
          But seeming so, for my particular end.
              (*Stabs body of Amadeo.*)
          Take that.
              (*Stabs body again.*)
          And there's for twitting me with treachery.

                    Exit Morelli.

Tertius. Sir, the absence of your father, the king,
          May not be understood. It may be thought
          By some, that know not why he is away,
          That wisdom, doubts, and mere dislike
          Of our proceedings kept the king from hence.

Cosimo. You strain too far, Lord Tertius.
          I rather of his absence make this use:
          It lends a lustre and more great opinion,
          A larger dare to our enterprise.

                    Exit Cosimo.

Tertius. Still all in vain comes counsel to his ear.

First Neapolitan Captain. That truth should be
          silent I had almost forgot.

Tertius. Men's faults do seldom to themselves appear;
          Their own transgressions partially they smother.

First Neapolitan Captain. You know his nature, that he's
          revengeful.

Tertius. Yes. And I know his sword
Hath a sharp edge: it's long and reaches far,
And where 'twill not extend, thither he darts it.

Exit All. Blackout.

ACT III

Scene 1

Before tent of Lucentio in a field outside Palermo.
Lucentio, seated, Camillo, Morelli, Lords, and Captains.

Morelli. I saw him in the battle range about;
    And watch'd him how he singled Naples forth.
    In single opposition, hand to hand,
    He did confound the best part of an hour
    In changing hardiment,
    Rendering faint quittance, wearied and out-breathed.

Camillo. His death, my liege, whose spirit lent a fire
    Even to the dullest peasant in his camp,
    Being bruited once, took fire and heat away
    From the best temper'd courage in his troops;
    For from his metal was his party steel'd;
    Which once in him abated, all the rest
    Turn'd on themselves, like dull and heavy lead:
    And as the thing that's heavy in itself,
    Upon enforcement flies with greatest speed,
    So did our men, heavy in the Prince's loss,
    Lend to this weight such lightness with their fear
    That arrows fled not swifter toward their aim
    Than did our soldiers, aiming at their safety,
    Fly from the field.

Soldiers carry in the bloody body of Amadeo on a litter
and set it before Lucentio.

Lucentio. O me! this sight of death is as bell,
    That warns my old age to a sepulcher.

Morelli. And is't not pity, O my grieved friends,
    That we, the sons and children of this isle,
    Were born to see so sad an hour as this.

Lucentio. Now let hot Aetna cool,
　　And be my heart an ever-burning hell!
　　These miseries are more than may be borne.

Camillo. Ah, that this sight should make so deep a wound,
　　And yet detested life not shrink thereat!
　　That ever death should let life bear his name,
　　Where life hath no more interest but to breathe!

Morelli. Hung be the heavens with black, yield day to
　　　　night!
　　Comets, importing change of times and states,
　　Brandish your crystal tresses in the sky,
　　And with them scourge the bad revolting stars.

Lucentio. O, let the vile world end,
　　And the premised flames of the last day
　　Knit earth and heaven together!
　　Now let the general trumpet blow his blast!
　　Had it pleased heaven
　　To try me with affliction; had they rain'd
　　All kinds of sores and shames on my bare head,
　　Steep'd me in poverty to the very lips,
　　Given to captivity me and my utmost hopes,
　　I should have found in some place of my soul
　　A drop of patience; of comfort no man speak:
　　Let's talk of graves, of worms, and epitaphs;
　　Make dust our paper and with rainy eyes
　　Write sorrow on the bosom of the earth,
　　Let's choose executors and talk of wills.

Morelli. Be moderate, be moderate.

Lucentio. Why tell you me of moderation?
　　The grief is fine, full, perfect, that I taste,
　　And violenteth in a sense as strong
　　As that which causeth it: how can I moderate it?

Morelli. Even so great men great losses should endure.

Camillo. My lord Morelli,
    The truth you speak doth lack some gentleness
    And time to speak it in.

Morelli. Honest plain words best pierce the ear of grief.

Camillo. You run the sore, when you should bring the
      plaster.

Lucentio. I pray thee, cease thy counsel,
    Which falls into mine ears as profitless
    As water in a sieve: give not me counsel;
    Nor let no comforter delight mine ear
    But such a one whose wrongs do suit with mine.
    Bring me a father that so loved his child,
    Whose joy of him is overwhelm'd like mine,
    And bid him speak of patience;
    Measure his woe the length and breadth of mine
    And let it answer every strain for strain,
    As thus for thus and such a grief for such,
    In every lineament, branch, shape, and form:
    If such a one will smile and stroke his beard,
    Bid sorrow wag, cry "hem!" when he should groan,
    Patch grief with proverbs; bring him yet to me,
    And I of him will gather patience.
    But there is no such man: for, brother, men
    Can counsel and speak comfort to that grief
    Which they themselves not feel; but, tasting it,
    Their counsel turns to passion.
    No, no; 'tis all men's office to speak patience
    To those that wring under the load of sorrow,
    But no man's virtue nor sufficiency
    To be so moral when he shall endure
    The like himself. Therefore give me no counsel:
    My griefs cry louder than advertisement.

Morelli. Therein do men from children nothing differ.

Lucentio. I pray thee, peace! I will be flesh and blood!

Camillo. Bear him from hence to the palace
        And the queen his mother. Peace be with him.

Soldiers carry Amadeo's body away. The rest begin to follow.

Morelli. Heaven hath a hand in these events,
        To whose high will we bound our calm contents.

Lucentio. O heavy hour!
        Methinks it should be now a huge eclipse
        Of sun and moon, and that the affrighted globe
        Should yawn at alteration.

Blackout.

ACT III

Scene 2

Palermo. Hall in royal palace. Adrianna, Sophia, Katrina, Lords, Duchess of Messina, and Ladies.

First Lord. My dear Queen Adrianna, I have words
That would be howl'd out in the desert air,
Where hearing should not latch them.
A heavier task could not have been imposed
Than I to speak my griefs unspeakable.

Adrianna. For god's sake, speak comfortable words.

First Lord. Should I do so, I should belie my thoughts:
Comfort's in heaven; and we are on the earth,
Where nothing lives but crosses, cares and grief.
Amadeo, your son, our prince, is dead.

Adrianna. It is not so; thou hast misspoke, misheard:
Be well advised, tell o'er thy tale again:
It cannot be; thou dost but say 'tis so:
I trust I may not trust thee; for thy word
Is but the vain breath of a common man:
Believe me, I do not believe thee, man.

First Lord. I crave thy highness' pardon.

Adrianna. This day, all things begun come to ill end,
Yea, faith itself to hollow falsehood change!

Katrina. Sister! Mother!

Adrianna. Give me no help in lamentation;
I am not barren to bring forth complaints;
All springs reduce their currents to mine eyes,
That I, being govern'd by the watery moon,
May send forth plenteous tears to drown the world!

Death, death; O amiable lovely death!
Thou odouriferous stench! sound rottenness!
Arise forth from the couch of lasting night,
Thou hate and terror to prosperity,
And I will kiss thy detestable bones
And put my eyeballs in thy vaulty brows
And ring these fingers with thy household worms
And stop this gap of breath with fulsome dust
And be a carrion monster like thyself.
Misery's love, O, come to me!

Duchess. You hold too heinous a respect for grief.

Adrianna. She speaks to me that never had a son.
Grief fills the room up of my absent son;
Then, have I reason to be fond of grief?
Fare you well: had you such a loss as I,
I could give better comfort than you do.
O Lord! My son, my Amadeo!
My life, my joy, my food, my all the world!

Duchess. Moderate lamentation is the right of the dead,
excessive grief the enemy to the living.

Adrianna. Oh, who shall hinder me to wail and weep,
To chide my fortune, and torment myself?
I'll join with black despair against my soul,
And to myself become an enemy.
Let my tears stanch the earth's dry appetite;
My son's sweet blood will make it shame and blush.

*Enter Lucentio and Camillo. Attendant provides stool for
Lucentio.*

Lucentio. Ay, my dear Queen; my heart is drown'd with
grief,
Whose flood begins to flow within mine eyes,
My body round engirt with misery.

Adrianna. Dead!
That gallant spirit hath aspired the clouds,

Which too untimely here did scorn the earth.
By his light did
All the chivalry of Sicily move
To do brave acts: he was indeed the glass
Wherein the noble youth did dress themselves:
He had no legs that practised not his gait;
In speech, in diet, in affections of delight,
In military rules, humours of blood,
He was the mark and glass, copy and book,
That fashion'd others. And him, O wondrous him!
O miracle of men! him did you leave,
Second to none, unseconded by you,
To look upon the hideous god of war
In disadvantage.

Sophia. Much is your sorrow; mine ten times so much!

Lucentio. Daughter, comfort your sister.

Katrina. Dearest Sophia,
    So much interest have I in thy sorrow
    As I had title in my noble brother.
    Do not seek to bear your griefs yourself;
    We all mourn with thee:
    O, could our mourning ease thy misery!

Sophia. O Katrina, that comfort comes too late;
    'Tis like a pardon after execution:
    Now I am past all comforts here, but prayers.
    O, now, for ever
    Farewell the tranquil mind! farewell content!
    My grief is so great
    That no supporter but the huge firm earth
    Can hold it up; here I and sorrows sit.

Duchess. Have done: some grief shows much of love;
    But much of grief shows still some want of wit.

Lucentio. Peace, Duchess!

Duchess.   I count it dangerous
     That she doth give her sorrow so much sway.

Lucentio.   Peace, I say, Duchess!

Sophia.   O, God, why do you make us love your goodly
         gifts,
     And snatch them straight away? My joy is death;
     Death, at whose name I oft have been afear'd,
     Because I wish'd this world's eternity.
     My heart, all mad with misery,
     Beats in this hollow prison of my flesh.

Duchess.   I have heard my granddam say full oft,
     Extremity of griefs would make us mad.

Lucentio.   Remove her!

            Ladies usher Duchess away.

Sophia.   I am not mad: I would to heaven I were!
     For then, 'tis like I should forget myself:
     O, if I could, what grief should I forget!
     Preach some philosophy to make me mad,
     For being not mad but sensible of grief,
     My reasonable part produces reason
     How I may be deliver'd of these woes,
     And teaches me to kill or hang myself:
     I am not mad; too well, too well I feel
     The different plague of each calamity.

*Soldiers carry in corpse of Amadeo, ready for burial, and
         set it before Lucentio and Adrianna.*

Lucentio.   This case of that huge spirit now is cold.

Sophia.   Now, by heaven,
     My blood begins my safer guides to rule;
     And passion, having my best judgment collied,
     Assays to lead the way.
     O heat, dry up my brains! tears seven times salt,
     Burn out the sense and virtue of mine eye!

For I am sick and capable of fears,
A widow, husbandless, subject to fears,
A woman, naturally born to fears.

Adrianna. God will revenge this; whom I will importune
With daily prayers all to that effect.

Lucentio. In peace and honour rest you my dead son,
Sicily's readiest champion, rest,
Secure from worldly chances and mishaps!
Here lurks no treason, here no envy swells,
Here grow no damned grudges; here are no storms,
No noise, but silence and eternal sleep.

Adrianna. Cursed be the hand that made these fatal holes!
Cursed be the heart that had the heart to do it!
Cursed the blood that let this blood from hence!
More direful hap betide that hated wretch,
That makes us wretched by the death of thee,
Than I can wish to adders, spiders, toads,
Or any creeping venom'd thing that lives!
If ever he have child, abortive be it,
Prodigious, and untimely brought to light,
Whose ugly and unnatural aspect
May fright the hopeful mother at the view;
And that be heir to his unhappiness!
If ever he have wife, let her be made
As miserable by the death of him
As I am made.

*Enter Cosimo, Tertius, and Captains. Cosimo kneels then
rises.*

Cosimo. The King of Naples, by his command,
To execute the charge he gave me,
Gives you all greetings that a king
Can send: and, but infirmity
Which waits upon worn times hath something seized
His wish'd ability, he had himself
The lands and waters 'twixt your throne and his
Measured to look upon you; he bade me say so.

I do also grieve to hear and do lament the
Sickness of King Lucentio.

Lucentio. Doth that grieve thee? Sir, grieve not on our
behalf.

Adrianna. Is this the scourge of Sicily? Cosimo,
The Prince of Naples, so much fear'd abroad
That with his name the mothers still their babes?
Foul devil, for God's sake, hence, and trouble us not;
For thou hast made the happy earth thy hell,
Fill'd it with cursing cries and deep exclaims.
O blood-bespotted Neapolitan,
If thou delight to view thy heinous deeds,
Behold this pattern of thy butcheries.
O God, which this blood madest, revenge his death!
O earth, which this blood drink'st revenge his death!
Either heaven with lightning strike the murderer dead,
Or earth, gape open wide and eat him quick,
As thou dost swallow up my good son's blood
Which his hell-govern'd arm hath butchered!

Cosimo. Thine eyes, sweet lady, have infected mine.

Adrianna. Would they were basilisks, to strike thee dead!

Cosimo. I would they were, that I might die at once;
For now they kill me with a living death.
Those eyes of thine from mine have drawn salt tears,
Shamed their aspect with store of childish drops:
These eyes that never shed remorseful tear.

Adrianna. To show an unfelt sorrow is an office
Which the false man does easy.
No doubt the murderous knife was dull and blunt
Till it was whetted on thy stone-cold heart.

Cosimo. Perhaps the lady hath
A fever with the absence of her son,
A madness, of which her life's in danger?

Adrianna. Can curses pierce the clouds and enter heaven?
　　Why, then, give way, dull clouds, to my quick curses!
　　If heaven have any grievous plague in store
　　Exceeding those that I can wish upon thee,
　　O, let them keep it till thy sins be ripe,
　　And then hurl down their indignation
　　On thee, the troubler of the poor world's peace.
　　The worm of conscience still begnaw thy soul!
　　Thy friends suspect for traitors while thou livest,
　　And take deep traitors for thy dearest friends!
　　No sleep close up that deadly eye of thine,
　　Unless it be whilst some tormenting dream
　　Affrights thee with a hell of ugly devils!
　　I conjure thee to leave me and be gone.
　　I have no moe sons for thee to murder.
　　Therefore take with thee my most heavy curse;
　　Which, in the day of battle, tire thee more
　　Than all the complete armour that thou wear'st!
　　My prayers on the adverse party fight;
　　Bloody thou art, bloody will be thy end;
　　Shame serves thy life and doth thy death attend.

Cosimo. Look, what is done cannot be now amended:
　　Men shall deal unadvisedly sometimes,
　　Which after hours give leisure to repent.

　　　　　　Adrianna begins to exit.

Sophia. O thou well skill'd in curses, stay awhile,
　　And teach me how to curse mine enemies!

Adrianna. Forbear to sleep the nights, and fast the days;
　　Compare dead happiness with living woe;
　　Think that thy babes were fairer than they were,
　　And he that slew them fouler than he is:
　　Bettering thy loss makes the bad causer worse:
　　Revolving this will teach thee how to curse.

Sophia. All the infections that the sun sucks up
　　From bogs, fens, flats, on Naples fall and make him
　　By inch-meal a disease!

And, sith there's no justice in earth nor hell,
We will solicit heaven and move our God
To send down Justice for to wreak our wrongs.

Cosimo. Enough of this. Things without remedy
     Should be without regard: what's done is done.
     Go, get thee hence.

     Exit Sophia, Adrianna, Katrina, and Ladies, following
     corpse borne by Soldiers. Tertius steps before Lucentio.

Tertius. King Pompeo and the Prince of Naples
     Doth will you, in the name of God Almighty,
     That you divest yourself, and bid you then resign
     Your crown and kingdom.

Lucentio. Must I give this heavy weight from off my head
     And this more heavy sceptre from my hand?

Tertius. Thou must.

Lucentio. (*Removing his crown.*) With a heavy heart, thus
     relinquish I
     The pride of kingly sway from out my heart;
     With mine own tears I wash away my balm,
     With mine own hands I give away my crown,
     With mine own tongue deny my sacred state,
     With mine own breath release all duty's rites.

     Lucentio hands crown to Tertius.

Tertius. For the King of Naples, Prince Cosimo
     Lays most lawful claim to this fair island.

Cosimo. If any here hold me a foe;
     If I unwittingly, or in my rage,
     Have aught committed that is hardly borne
     By any in this presence, I desire
     To reconcile me to his friendly peace:
     'Tis death to me to be at enmity;

I hate it, and desire all good men's love.
I thank my God for my humility.

Morelli enters and goes to stand among Neapolitans.

Lucentio. (*Aside to Camillo.*) Is this our brother, Duke of
    Messina?

Camillo. Yea, he's gone to serve the Prince of Naples.

Lucentio. Boiling choler chokes
    The hollow passage of my poison'd voice.

Cosimo. Know that we institute the Duke of Messina
    To be our regent in these parts.

Lucentio. O villain, viper, damn'd without redemption!
    Dog, easily won to fawn on any man!
    Snake, in my heart-blood warm'd, that stings my heart!
    You sign your place and calling, in full seeming,
    With meekness and humility; but your heart
    Is cramm'd with arrogancy, spleen, and pride.
    You have, by fortune and the prince's favours,
    Gone slightly o'er low steps and now are mounted
    Where powers are your retainers.

Camillo. Treacherous Morelli, brother, thou art
    Not fit to govern and rule multitudes;
    That head of thine doth not become a crown.

Cosimo. (*To Lucentio.*) Sir, you have a daughter, call'd
    Katrina,
    Virtuous and fair, royal and gracious.
    I have perused her well;
    Her virtues graced with external gifts
    Do breed love's settled passions in my heart:
    And like as rigor of tempestuous gusts
    Provokes the mightiest hulk against the tide,
    So am I driven by breath of her renown
    Either to suffer shipwreck or arrive
    Where I may have fruition of her love.

Beauty and honour in her are so mingled
That they have caught my heart.
Then know, that from my soul I love thy daughter.
And mean to make her Princess of Naples.

Lucentio almost swoons. Camillo steadies him. Cosimo
smirks.

Morelli. Brother Lucentio, consider this:
To hold you in perpetual amity,
To make you kinsmen, and to knit your hearts
With an unslipping knot, take Cosimo
Katrina to his wife; whose beauty claims
No worse a husband than the best of men;
Whose virtue and whose general graces speak
That which none else can utter. By this marriage,
All great fears, which now import their dangers,
Would then be nothing: truths would be tales,
Where now half tales be truths: her love to both
Would, each to other and all loves to both,
Draw after her.

Cosimo. Old Lucentio, I always thought
It was both impious and unnatural
That such immanity and bloody strife
Should reign among professors of one faith.

Lucentio. These times of woe afford no time to woo.
How canst thou?

Cosimo. That would I learn of you,
As one that are acquainted with her humour.

Lucentio. And wilt thou learn of me?

Cosimo. Sire, with all my heart.

Lucentio. Send to her, by the man that slew her brother,
A freshly bleeding-heart; thereon engrave
"Amadeo"; then haply she will weep:
Therefore present to her

            A handkerchief; which, say to her, did drain
            The purple sap from her sweet brother's body
            And bid her dry her weeping eyes therewith.
            If this inducement force her not to love,
            Send her a story of thy noble acts.

Cosimo. Come, come, you mock me; this is not the way
            To win your daughter.

Lucentio. There is no other way.

Cosimo. Say that I did all this for love of her.

Lucentio. Nay, then indeed she cannot choose but hate
            thee,
         Having bought love with such a bloody spoil.

Cosimo. If I did take the kingdom from your son,
            To make amends, I'll give it to your daughter.
            I will beget
            Mine issue of your blood upon your daughter.
            The loss you have is but a son being king,
            And by that loss your daughter is made queen.
            I cannot make you what amends I would,
            Therefore accept such kindness as I can.
            Go with her mother, to thy daughter go;
            Make bold her bashful years with your experience;
            Prepare her ears to hear a wooer's tale;
            Put in her tender heart the aspiring flame
            Of golden sovereignty; acquaint the princess
            With the sweet silent hours of marriage joys.

Lucentio. What were I best to say? her brother's killer
            Would be her lord?
            Under what title shall I woo for thee,
            That God, the law, my honour and her love,
            Can make seem pleasing to her tender years?

Cosimo. Infer Sicily's peace by this alliance.
            Say that the prince, which may command, entreats.
            Say, she shall be a high and mighty queen.

Say, I will love her everlastingly,
Sweetly in force unto her fair life's end.
Say, I, her sovereign, am her subject love.
Be eloquent in my behalf to her.

Lucentio. Never. My reasons are too deep and dead.

Cosimo. Harp not on that string, sire; that is past.

Lucentio. Harp on it still shall I till heart-strings break.

Cosimo. Be opposite all planets of good luck
  To my proceedings, if
  I tender not thy beauteous princely daughter!
  In her consists my happiness and thine!

Morelli. Brother, the sooner to effect
  And surer bind this knot of amity,
  Proffer you your daughter to his lordship
  In marriage, with a large and sumptuous dowry.
  Peace it bodes, and love and quiet life.

  Lucentio, weakened, stands up with difficulty.

Cosimo. What's the matter? How fares my gracious sir?

Lucentio. Thy proposed match doth
  Join with the present sickness that I have.

Cosimo. Sit thee down, sir.

Lucentio. Shall I be tempted by the devil thus?
  Shall I forget myself to myself?

Cosimo. Bear her my true love's kiss.

Lucentio. But woo her, cruel Naples, get her heart,
  My will to her consent is but a part.

Cosimo. We were not born to sue, but to command.
  Whatsoever I did bid thee do,
  Thou shouldst attempt it.

Now will we take some order in the town,
Placing therein some expert officers;
Much more, in this great work,
Which is almost to pluck a kingdom down
And set another up, should we survey;
And then depart to Naples and the king.

Exit Cosimo, Tertius, and Captains.

Camillo. Sir, this most cruel usage of your daughter
Will ignoble make you,
Yea, scandalous to the world.

Lucentio. But in this troublous time what's to be done?
We must learn, Camillo,
To think our former state a happy dream;
From which awaked, the truth of what we are
Shows us but this: I am sworn brother
To grim Necessity, and he and I
Will keep a league till death.

Camillo. There is no more mercy in Cosimo than there is
milk in a male tiger; that shall our poor country find.
It is not possible, it cannot be,
Naples should keep his word in loving us;
Look how we can, or sad or merrily,
Interpretation will misquote our looks,
And we shall feed like oxen at a stall,
The better cherish'd, still the nearer death.

Lucentio. Our lands, our lives and all are Cosimo's,
And nothing can we call our own but death
And that small model of the barren earth
Which serves as paste and cover to our bones.
For God's sake, let us sit upon the ground
And tell sad stories of the death of kings.

Camillo. All comfort go with thee!

Blackout.

ACT III

Scene 3

Palermo. A room in the royal palace. Cosimo.

Cosimo. I burn, I pine, I perish,
  If I achieve not this young modest girl.
  Hear my prayers
  You gods that made me man, and sway in love,
  That have inflamed desire in my breast
  To taste the fruit of yon celestial tree,
  Be my helps,
  As I am son and servant to your will,
  To compass such a boundless happiness!

Enter Morelli with Katrina.

Cosimo. Princess, I would speak with you.
  As thy father told you,
  You and I shall be married.

Katrina. The duke my uncle is to blame for this.

Cosimo. Sweet Princess Katrina,
  In love the heavens themselves do guide the state;
  Money buys lands, but wives are sold by fate.

She looks scornfully at him.

Cosimo. (*Cont'd.*) Teach not thy lips such scorn, for they
      were made
  For kissing, lady, not for such contempt.
  I never sued to friend nor enemy;
  My tongue could never learn sweet smoothing words;
  But, now thy beauty is proposed my fee,
  My proud heart sues, and prompts my tongue to
      speak.

Katrina. Dissembling, detested, soulless villain.

Cosimo. Touch but my lips with those fair lips of thine—
    The kiss shall be thine own as well as mine.
    What seest thou in the ground? hold up thy head:
    Look in mine eye-balls, there thy beauty lies;
    Then why not lips on lips, since eyes in eyes?

    Cosimo approaches Katrina and she backs away.

Katrina. 'Tis time to fear when tyrants seem to kiss.

Cosimo. Why, look you, how you storm!
    I would be friends with you and have your love.
    'Tis the curse in love, and still approved,
    That women cannot love where they're beloved!
    Yet I hold you as a thing ensky'd and sainted.
    And to be talk'd with in sincerity,
    As with a saint.

Katrina. Hateful, brutish, abominable, murderous villain!

Cosimo. Were I hard-favour'd, foul, or wrinkled-old,
    Ill-nurtured, crooked, churlish, harsh in voice,
    O'erworn, despised, rheumatic and cold,
    Thick-sighted, barren, lean and lacking juice,
    Then mightst thou pause, for then I were not for thee;
    But having no defects, why dost abhor me?

Katrina. You did kill my brother!

Cosimo. Not I.

Katrina. Falsehood is worse in princes than beggars.

Cosimo. They say, best men are molded out of faults;
    And, for the most, become much more the better
    For being a little bad.

Katrina. Damned insolent, smiling, craven villain.

Cosimo. Still, I swear I love you.

Katrina. If you but said so, 'twere as deep with me:
    If you swear still, your recompense is still
    That I regard it not.

Cosimo. This is no answer. I said I love you.

Katrina. But that you shall not say I yield being silent,
    I would not speak. I pray you, spare me.
    And learn now, for all, I do here pronounce,
    By the very truth of it, I hate you.

Cosimo. Will it be ever thus? Ungracious wretch.
    (*Aside.*) But hold.
    Foul words and frowns must not repel a lover;
    What though the rose have prickles, yet 'tis pluck'd:
    Were beauty under twenty locks kept fast,
    Yet love breaks through and picks them all at last.
             (*To Katrina.*)
    Maids, in modesty, say "no" to that
    Which they would have the profferer construe "ay."

Katrina. Men may construe things after their fashion,
    Thou damned, indistinguishable cur!

Cosimo. You uncivil lady,
    To whose ingrate and unauspicious altars
    My soul the faithfull'st offerings hath breathed out
    That e'er devotion tender'd!
    Thou art obdurate, flinty, hard as steel,
    Nay, more than flint, for stone at rain relenteth.
    Art thou a woman, and canst not feel
    What 'tis to love? How want of love tormenteth?
    To tell thee plain, I aim to lie with thee.

Katrina. To tell you plain, I had rather lie in prison.
    The baser is it, coming from a prince,
    To shame your hope with deeds degenerate:
    The mightier man, the mightier is the thing
    That makes him honour'd, or begets him hate.

Cosimo. (*Aside.*) She speaks poniards, and every word
    stabs.
    What though I killed her brother.
    The readiest way to make the wretch amends
    Is to become her husband: the which I will.
           (*To Katrina.*)
    It stands agreed with your father.
    You sin against obedience, which you owe him.
           (*To Morelli.*)
    Call him hither.

    Exit Morelli. Cosimo struts around.

Cosimo. To cross me from the golden time I look for!
    Why, this it is, when men are ruled by women.
    Disdain and scorn ride sparkling in her eyes,
    Misprising what they look on; she cannot love,
    Nor take no shape nor project of affection,
    She is so self-endeared.
    I'll tame her; I'll bring her in subjection.
           (*To Katrina.*)
    Come what may, I do adore thee so.

Katrina. I had rather be married to a death's-head with a
    bone in his mouth.

*Re-enter Morelli with Lucentio, feeble, assisted by Camillo
and Adrianna.*

Cosimo. Here comes your father; tell him so yourself,
    And see how he will take it.

Lucentio. How now, what's the matter?

Katrina. 'Tis a villain, sir, I do not love to look on.

Cosimo. Father, plead my passions for Katrina's love.

Lucentio. Katrina, thou better know'st
    The offices of nature, bond of childhood,
    Dues of gratitude.

Katrina. Father, I cannot love him.

Adrianna. (*To Lucentio.*) I do shame
  To think of what a noble strain you are,
  And of how coward a spirit.

Katrina. I pray you, Father, I will not marry yet.

Cosimo. Either frame your will to mine, be ruled by me,
  Or I will make you.
  When I return from Italy,
  The rites of marriage shall be solemnized.

Adrianna. O, it is excellent
  To have a giant's strength; but it is tyrannous
  To use it like a giant.

Katrina. My very soul abhors thee!

Cosimo. Indeed! Very well!
  Fair glass of light, I loved you, and could still,
  But I must tell you, now my thoughts revolt.
  Thou art disobedient, forward, lacking duty,
  Peevish, sullen, stubborn and proud.
  'Tis beauty that doth oft make women proud;
  But, God he knows, thy share thereof is small:
  'Tis virtue that doth make them most admired;
  The contrary doth make thee wonder'd at:
  'Tis government that makes them seem divine;
  The want thereof makes thee abominable:
  Women are soft, mild, pitiful and flexible;
  Thou stern, obdurate, flinty, rough, remorseless.
  Good sooth, I care not for you.
  This pride of yours hath drawn my love from you.

Katrina. Amen to that!
  For me, I am the mistress of my fate!

Exit Katrina, Adrianna, and Lucentio assisted by Camillo.

Cosimo. I will conclude to hate her, nay, indeed,
  To be revenged upon her.

Morelli. Let her go, my liege.
  What is wedlock forced but a hell,
  An age of discord and continual strife?
  Whereas the contrary bringeth bliss,
  And is a pattern of celestial peace.
  I have a daughter, sir, called Lucinda,
  Obedient, virtuous, chaste, and fair.
  In our opinions she should be preferr'd.
  Shall I call her in?

  Exit Morelli. Cosimo struts around some more.

Cosimo. There is no woman's sides
  Can bide the beating of so strong a passion
  As love doth give my heart; no woman's heart
  So big, to hold so much; they lack retention;
  Alas, their love may be call'd appetite,
  No motion of the liver, but the palate,
  That suffer surfeit, cloyment and revolt;
  But mine is all as hungry as the sea,
  And can digest as much: make no compare
  Between that love a woman can bear me
  And that I owe a woman.

  Re-enter Morelli with Duchess, leading Lucinda.

Morelli. Prince Cosimo, may it please your grace,
  My daughter, Lucinda.

Cosimo. How now, young maid, how dost thou?

Morelli. The valiant Prince seeks you for his love.
  What say you? can you love the gentleman?
  Read o'er the volume of the Prince's face,
  And find delight writ there with beauty's pen;
  Examine every married lineament,
  And see how one another lends content,
  And what obscured in this fair volume lies

Find written in the margent of his eyes.
So shall you share all that he doth possess,
By having him, making yourself no less.

Lucinda. Please, I beg of you, father. Pardon me.

Morelli. Lucinda, daughter!

Lucinda. Call you me daughter? now, I promise you
You have show'd a tender fatherly regard,
To wish me wed to one so sinister.
O bid me leap, rather than marry him,
From off the battlements of yonder tower;
Or walk in thievish ways; or bid me lurk
Where serpents are; chain me with roaring bears;
Or shut me nightly in a charnel-house,
O'er cover'd quite with dead men's rattling bones,
With reeky shanks and yellow chapless skulls;
Or bid me go into a new-made grave
And hide me with a dead man in his shroud;
And I will do it without fear or doubt,
To live an unstain'd maid for my sweet love.

Duchess and Morelli. (*Together.*) Thy sweet love? Thy
sweet love?
Prithee, who is he that thou mean'st?
Is he a prince, the son of King Pompeo?

Cosimo. Enough of this.

Exit Cosimo.

Duchess. You a daughter!

Morelli. Dost not count thyself blest,
Unworthy as thou art, that we have wrought
So worthy a gentleman to be thy bridegroom?

Lucinda. Good father, I beseech you on my knees,
Hear me with patience but to speak a word.

Morelli. Hang thee, young baggage! disobedient wretch!
I tell thee what: learn to love the Prince,
Or never after look me in the face:
Speak not, reply not, do not answer me.
God's bread! it makes me mad:
Day, night, hour, tide, time, work, play,
Alone, in company, still my care hath been
To have her match'd: and having now provided
A gentleman of noble parentage,
Proportion'd as one's thought would wish a man;
And then to have a wretched puling fool,
A whining mammet, in her fortune's tender,
To answer "I pray you, pardon me."
But, as you will not wed, I'll pardon you:
Graze where you will, you shall not house with me.

Exit All.

ACT III

Scene 4

Burgundy. Before Valmond's castle. Enter Musik and
Pierre from different directions.

Pierre. Monsieur Musik. How goes it now, sir?
   What news abroad i' the world?

Musik. None, Pierre, but that there is so great a fever on
   goodness, that the dissolution of it must cure it:
   novelty is only in request; and it is as dangerous to be
   aged in any kind of course, as it is virtuous to be
   constant in any undertaking. There is scarce truth
   enough alive to make societies secure; but security
   enough to make fellowships accurst: This news is old
   enough, yet it is every day's news.

Pierre. Ah, my good friend,
   Thou art not for the fashion of these times.
   Give me that man, as thou art to thyself,
   That is not passion's slave, and I will wear him
   In my heart's core, ay, in my heart of heart,
   As I do thee.

Enter Valmond.

Valmond. Well met, honest gentlemen. Monsieur Pierre,
   Monsieur Musik. Good day to both of you.

Pierre. Good day, my lord. I crave your pardon.
   My present business calls me from you.
   I commend you to your own content.

Exit Pierre.

Valmond. He that commends me to mine own content
   Commends me to the thing I cannot get.

Musik. So far from cheer and from your former state?
　　What is the matter with thee?

Valmond. Happiness courts me in her best array;
　　But, like a misbehaved and sullen wench,
　　I pout'st upon my fortune.

Musik. My Lord,
　　I would you would make use of that good wisdom
　　Whereof I know you are fraught, and put away
　　These dispositions that of late transform you
　　From what you rightly are.

Valmond. And so would I; yet I know not how.
　　Methinks, sir, the spirit of my father, which I think is
　　within me, begins to mutiny against this melancholy.
　　Bestow your counsels on me, if't please you;
　　What would you do, Monsieur Musik?

Musik. I should honour the greatness of his name.

Valmond. How would you show this honour?

Musik. Let me ask: What would you undertake
　　To show yourself your father's son in deed
　　More than in words?

Valmond. I know not.

Musik. Let's think.
　　Would you undertake to study fashions
　　To adorn your body? Would you be a scholar of music,
　　instruments and poetry?
　　Would you study for the people's welfare?
　　Would you debate of commonwealth affairs?
　　Would you build churches? Erect a tomb?
　　Build a statue to make him glorious?
　　Ah ha!
　　I have a young conception in my brain:
　　How stands your disposition to be married?

Valmond. Why ask you this?

Musik. Torches are made to light, jewels to wear:
     Thou wast begot; to get it is thy duty.
     Upon the earth's increase why shouldst thou feed,
     Unless the earth with thy increase be fed?
     By law of nature thou art bound to breed.
     She carved thee for her seal, and meant thereby
     Thou should'st print more, not let that copy die.

Valmond. I do confess, I have considered of it.

Musik. But where would you
     Bestow your love and your affections?

Valmond. What think'st thou of Princess Katrina?

Musik. If lusty love should go in quest of beauty,
     Where should he find it fairer than in her?
     If zealous love should go in search of virtue,
     Where should he find it purer than in her?
     If love ambitious sought a match of birth,
     Whose veins bound richer blood than Katrina's?
     Such as she is, in beauty, virtue, birth,
     Is the young Princess every way complete.
     Come, come, disclose the state of your affection.

Valmond. I never shouldst love woman like to her;
     With her beauty and her wit,
     Her affability and bashful modesty,
     Her wondrous qualities and mild behavior.
     Who sees the heavenly Katrina
     That, like a rude and savage man of Ind,
     At the first opening of the gorgeous east,
     Bows not his vassal head and strucken blind
     Kisses the base ground with obedient breast?
     What peremptory eagle-sighted eye
     Dares look upon the heaven of her brow,
     That is not blinded by her majesty?
     This is a creature,
     Would she begin a sect, might quench the zeal

Of all professors else, make proselytes
Of who she but bid follow.

Musik. But what warmth is there in her affection towards
you?

Valmond. When yet we were in Sicily,
Though I was then frugal of my mirth,
As, I confess, it is my nature's plague,
In jest
Oft did she but sweetly chide me for faults.
Yet at my parting sweetly did she smile
And gave me this.

    Valmond shows him the chain around his neck.

Musik. This shows a sound affection. Come, sir, come;
Make use of time, let not advantage slip.
What would you say to Princess Katrina?

Valmond. I would say how I have been transformed;
That I have turn'd away my former self.

Musik. Nay. Tush, tush! Thou foolish youth!
Write to her a love-line; in plain terms
Tell her your loving tale; make much ado about
nothing, or what you will, as you like it;
For never anything can be amiss,
When simpleness and duty tender it,
And all's well that ends well.

    Enter Beauchance and Messenger in haste.

Valmond. What's the matter, Count?

Beauchance. A messenger with letters from Sicily.

    Messenger gives Valmond some letters.

Beauchance. Now, Duke, what news?

Valmond. O most horrid, heinous, and obscene!
     Naples hath made a conquest of Sicily;
     King Lucentio is exceeding ill;
     The Duke of Messina, his substitute,
     Advanced to great and high estate,
     Is left to govern;
     Prince Cosimo is promised to be wived
     To fair Katrina. To be married! Alas!

Musik. The policy of that purpose made more in the
     marriage than the love of the parties.

Beauchance. Courage, Valmond! The fair princess loves
        thee;
     She is a theme of honour and renown,
     A spur to valiant and magnanimous deeds.

Valmond. (*Looking at another letter.*)
     O woful day! most lamentable day!
     Amadeo, my dear friend, slain in battle!
     I cannot weep; for all my body's moisture
     Scarce serves to quench my furnace-burning heart.

Musik. Give sorrow words: the grief that does not speak
     Whispers the o'er-fraught heart and bids it break.

Valmond. Why should calamity be full of words?

Musik. Poor breathing orators of miseries!
     Let them have scope: though what they do impart
     Help not all, yet do they ease the heart.

Valmond. My tongue cannot unload my heart's great
        burthen;
     For selfsame wind that I should speak withal
     Is kindling coals that fires all my breast,
     And burns me up with flames that tears would quench.
     To weep is to make less the depth of grief:
     Tears then for babes; blows and revenge for me.

Beauchance. Let's make us medicines of our great
      revenge,
    To cure this deadly grief.

Valmond. If this news be true, I feel me much to blame,
    So idly to profane the precious time.
    I firmly am resolved they shall have aid.
    My purse, my person, my extremest means
    Lie all unlock'd to their occasions.
    Bear with me; I am hungry for revenge;
    Amadeo, I am Revenge, sent to work
    Vengeance and confusion on thy foes.

Beauchance. Be this the whetstone of your sword: let grief
    Convert to anger; blunt not the heart, enrage it.

Valmond. (*To Messenger.*) Come, thou shalt bear a letter
    to them straight.

Exit Valmond and Messenger.

Musik. I would not be a Neapolitan, of all nations; I had as
    lieve be a condemned man.

Beauchance. Lucinda, I return to you again.
    At last, now shall I see my love, my wife.

Exit.

ACT III

Scene 5

Palermo. A room in the palace. Adrianna and Camillo in mourning. Enter Cosimo, Morelli, and Tertius.

Cosimo. How doth the king?

Adrianna. Exceeding well. His cares are now all ended.

Cosimo. I hope, not dead.

Camillo. He's walked the way of nature.
    The life of all his blood is touch'd corruptibly,
    And to our purposes he lives no more.

Cosimo. We grieve to hear't.
    What faults he made before the last, I think
    Might have found easy fines.
    Lady, we will mourn with thee:
    Could our mourning but ease thy misery.
    Sorrow so royally in you appears
    That I will deeply put the fashion on
    And wear it in my heart.

Adrianna. So ridest thou triumphing in my woe.

Cosimo. Unkind abuse; in despite of this scorn,
    According to his virtue let us use him,
    With all respect and rites of burial.
    Then, ourself, Lord Tertius, and the rest,
    After some respite will return to Messina,
    From thence to Italy.
    Perhaps, when I return, young Katrina
    Shall I happily make a joyful bride.

Exit Camillo and Adrianna.

Cosimo. Now for our other business.

      Morelli beckons and Cambio enters.

Morelli. My Lord, in Cambio you shall find here
    A man who is the abstract of all faults
    That all men follow. I assure thee there is not one so
    young and so villainous this day living.

Cambio. I thank you; I am not of many words, but I thank
      you.
    'Twill vex thy soul to hear what I shall speak;
    For I must talk of abominable deeds,
    Complots of mischief, treason, villainies
    Ruthful to hear.

Cosimo. I am myself indifferent honest; but yet I could
    accuse me of such things that it were better my mother
    had not borne me: I am very proud, revengeful,
    ambitious, with more offences at my beck than I have
    thoughts to put them in. What should such fellows as
    we do crawling between earth and heaven? We are
    arrant knaves, all.

Cambio. If one good deed in all my life I did,
    I do repent it from my very soul.

Cosimo. Art thou not sorry for these heinous deeds?

Cambio. Ay, that I had not done a thousand more.
    Even now I curse the day—and yet, I think,
    Few come within the compass of my curse—
    Wherein I did not some notorious ill,
    As ravish a maid, or plot the way to do it,
    Accuse some innocent and forswear myself,
    Set deadly enmity between two friends,
    Set fire on barns and hay-stacks in the night.
    Oft have I digg'd up dead men from their graves,
    And set them upright at their dear friends' doors,
    Even when their sorrows almost were forgot;
    And on their skins, as on the bark of trees,

Have with my knife carved in Roman letters,
"Let not your sorrow die, though I am dead."
Tut, I have done a thousand dreadful things
As willingly as one would kill a fly,
And nothing grieves me heartily indeed
But that I cannot do ten thousand more.
Had I power, I should
Pour the sweet milk of concord into hell,
Uproar the universal peace, confound
All unity on earth.

Cosimo.   Verily, a detestable villain.
      You are come to me in a happy time;
      The rather for I have some sport in hand
      Wherein your cunning can assist me much.

Cambio.   What you bid me undertake,
      Though that my death were adjunct to my act,
      By heaven, I would do it.

Cosimo.   I tell thee, my friend,
      Your face is as a book where men
      May read strange matters.
      False face must hide what the false heart doth know.
      Come, fellow, canst thou change thy colour?

Cambio.   Tut, I can counterfeit
      At any time, to grace my stratagems.
      Ornament is but the seeming truth
      Which cunning times put on to entrap the wisest.

Cosimo.   Good fellow, shall I tell you a thing?
      The Princess Katrina
      Hath despised me rejoicingly, and I'll
      Be merry in my revenge.

Cambio.   They say she does refuse to marry thee.

Cosimo.   Note me:
      Good name in man and woman, dear my sir,
      Is the immediate jewel of their souls:

Who steals my purse steals trash; 'tis something,
        nothing;
'Twas mine, 'tis his, and has been slave to thousands:
But he that filches from me my good name
Robs me of that which not enriches him
And makes me poor indeed.
The purest treasure mortal times afford
Is spotless reputation; that away—
Do you note me?
They say Katrina is an earthly paragon;
But no perfection is so absolute
That some impurity doth not pollute.
In your service to Duke Morelli,
Frame yourself
To orderly soliciting, and be friended
With aptness of the season. Take root
By the fair weather that you make yourself.
In good time, urge her hateful luxury
And bestial appetite in change of lust;
Which stretches to the servants, husbands, sons,
Even where her lustful eye or savage heart,
Without control, listed to make her prey.
Whisper abroad:
"She's but the sign and semblance of her honour.
Behold how like a maid she blushes here!
Would you not swear,
All you that see her, that she were a maid,
By these exterior shows? But she is none:
She knows the heat of a luxurious bed;
Her blush is guiltiness, not modesty."
Do you mark me, sir?

Cambio. Excellent! My thoughts are ripe in mischief.
        Your lordship's a goodly villain.

Cosimo. Fare you well now, sir.

Cambio. (*Exiting.*) O, how this villainy
        Doth fat me with the very thoughts of it!
        What other pleasure can the world afford?

Exit Cambio.

Tertius. This strained passion doth you wrong, my lord.

Cosimo. Tertius, I do observe you now of late:
    I have not from your eyes that gentleness
    And show of love as I was wont to have.
         (*To Morelli.*)
    Duke Morelli of Messina, you have
    Served us well. We heartily solicit
    Your gracious self to take on you the charge
    And kingly government of this your land,
    As our protector, steward, substitute.
    In our remove be thou at full ourself.
    As deputy, your scope is as mine own,
    So to enforce or qualify the laws.

Morelli. Most gracious Prince, your love deserves
    my thanks.

Cosimo. We shall write to you
    As time and our concernings shall importune,
    How it goes with us, and do look to know
    What doth befall you here. So, fare you well.
    To the hopeful execution do I leave you
    Of your commissions.

Exit Cosimo and Morelli.

Tertius. Alack, when once our grace we have forgot,
    Nothing goes right: we would, and we would not.
    Happy star reign now.

Exit. Blackout.

ACT III

Scene 6

*Palermo. Room in Morelli's house. Lucinda reading
letter. Katrina sewing. Enter Duchess of Messina.*

Duchess. How now! what letter are you reading there?

Lucinda. May't please my lady, 'tis a word or two
Of commendations sent from a friend.

Duchess. Lend me the letter; let me see what news.

Lucinda. There's no news, madam, but that she writes
How happily she lives.

Duchess. Come, girl, what letters had you late from
France?

Duchess pulls letter out of Lucinda's hand and reads it.

Duchess. What's here?
A letter, that you love the Count Beauchance!

Enter Morelli.

Morelli. How now? What's the matter?

Duchess. Seest thou this letter? take it up, I pray thee.
Read here.
Your daughter, if you have not given her leave,
Hath made a gross revolt;
Tying her duty, beauty, wit and fortunes
In an extravagant and wheeling stranger.
She tells us here, she's wed the stranger knight!

Morelli. O she deceives me past thought!
You are married? What say you, daughter?
Speak! Speak! Fie, fie upon her!

There's language in her eye, her cheek, her lip,
Nay, her foot speaks.

Lucinda. 'Tis true. I am in love with Count Beauchance.

Duchess. You speak like a green girl.

Lucinda. I am a married woman.

Duchess. Where is thy husband now?

Morelli. O treason of the blood! Who would be a father!
Fathers, from hence trust not your daughters' minds
By what you see them act. Is there not charms
By which the property of youth and maidhood
May be abused? O, my daughter!
The man hath bewitch'd the bosom of my child;
And stolen the impression of her fantasy.
With cunning hath he filch'd my daughter's heart.
She is abused, stol'n from me, and corrupted
By spells and medicines bought of mountebanks;
For nature so preposterously to err,
Being not deficient, blind, or lame of sense,
Sans witchcraft could not.
The foul thief hath enchanted her.

Katrina. Let me speak and lay a sentence,
Which, as a grise or step, may help.

Morelli. I pray thee, thou fool, speak not!

Duchess. How sharper than a serpent's tooth it is
To have a thankless child!

Lucinda. Good father, I beseech you on my knees—

Morelli. Daughter, be gone! I will not hear thy vain excuse;
As thou lovest thy life, make speed from hence.
Thou basest thing, avoid! hence, from my sight!
Thou'rt poison to my blood.
Hence from Palermo art thou banished!

Katrina. Pronounce that sentence then on me, my liege:
    I cannot live without her company.

Morelli. You! You are a fool.
    Thy infamy is rumour'd through the town,
    And thou art scandalous to the world.
    Ay, but thou shalt not go: the Prince desires thee.

        Exit Morelli and Duchess.

Katrina. I pray; weep not, coz, all things shall be well.

Lucinda. But I am banished!

Katrina. I shall go with thee. Listen, fair cousin:
    I live scandalized and foully spoken of.
    A recreant and most degenerate traitor
    Doth rumour it abroad I am unchaste;
    Myself on every post proclaimed a strumpet.
    I am disgraced, impeach'd and baffled here,
    Pierced to the soul with slander's venom'd spear;
    I will go with thee for mine own escape.

Lucinda. Whither shall we go?

Katrina. To seek our uncle, worthy Camillo,
    Gone already to Syracusa.
    My mother and Sophia shall come too.

Lucinda. Devise the fittest time and safest way
    To hide us from pursuit that will be made.

Katrina. Steal forth thy father's house tonight,
    And in the wood, a league without the town,
    There will we stay for thee.

Lucinda. Yes, yes! Let's away,
    And get our jewels and our wealth together.

Katrina. O Lucinda, how happily I bear
    Me hence from forth the noise and rumour.

Your love and pity doth the impression fill
Which vulgar scandal stamp'd upon my brow.

Lucinda. Now go we in consent
To liberty and not to banishment.

Exit. Blackout.

ACT IV

Scene 1

Syracuse. Palace of Duke Camillo. Camillo, Adrianna,
Katrina, Lucinda, and Lords.

First Lord. We have descried, upon our neighbouring
          shore,
     A portly sail of ships make hitherward
     To Syracusa; by the semblance
     Of their white flags displayed, they bring us peace,
     And come to us as favourers, not as foes.

          Enter Messenger. He hands a letter to Camillo.

Messenger. My gracious sovereign, as I rode from the
          port,
     A letter was deliver'd to my hands.

Camillo. I learn by this that the Duke of Burgundy,
     Comes here this night to Syracusa.
     Thirty tall ships, ten thousand men of war,
     Are making hither with all due expedience.

Messenger. He is very near by this: he was not three
          leagues
     Off when I left him.

Katrina. Now, dear mother, our hopes are answered.
     Our expectation hath this day an end.

Adrianna. Oft expectation hits
     Where hope is coldest and despair most fits.

Lucinda. And the County Beauchance?
     Can he be here in person? 'tis impossible!

Adrianna. Impossible be strange attempts to those
  That weigh their pains in sense and do suppose
  What hath been cannot be.

Lucinda. I am giddy; expectation whirls me round.
  The imaginary relish is so sweet
  That it enchants my sense: what will it be,
  When that the watery palate tastes indeed
  Love's thrice repured nectar?

  Enter Valmond, Musik, and Beauchance. They kneel to
       Adrianna.

Valmond. Your highness, Queen Adrianna,
  We have heard your miseries as far as France;
  To your most royal person, we hither come
  Even at your feet to lay our arms and power,
  And to relieve you of your heavy load.
  In all submission and humility
  We do present ourselves unto your highness.

Adrianna. You are come by miracle.

Valmond. Mourning the deaths of the prince and the king,
  Know that our griefs are risen to the top,
  And now at length they overflow their banks.
  Might liquid tears or heart-offending groans
  Or blood-consuming sighs recall their lives,
  I would be blind with weeping, sick with groans,
  Look pale as primrose with blood-drinking sighs,
  And all to have these noble friends alive.
  Here on my knee I vow to God above,
  I'll never pause again, never stand still,
  Never taste the pleasures of the world,
  Never be infected with delight,
  Nor conversant with ease and idleness,
  Till either death hath closed these eyes of mine
  Or I on Naples rain hot vengeance.

Adrianna. We thank you, valiant Duke, and bid you
  Most welcome. We shall remain your debtor.

Valmond. The service and the loyalty I owe,
 In doing it, pays itself. Your highness' part
 Is to receive our duties; and our duties
 Are to your throne and state children.

Adrianna. You owe little duty; we owe thee much,
 And do honour thee.

Valmond. We do not look for reverence, but to love.
 Duke Camillo,
 Let our ships and number of our men
 Be like a beacon fired to amaze your eyes.

Camillo. Your grace is welcome to our town and us.
 How far off lies your power?

Musik. Hard by, my gracious lord;
 Thou shalt have ten thousand fighting men!

                Enter Messenger with letter for Camillo.

Camillo. By this intelligence we learn Cosimo
 And the army of Naples are lately landed.
 By Morelli, his corrupt deputy,
 The commons hath he pill'd with grievous taxes,
 And quite lost their hearts; the nobles hath he fined
 For ancient quarrels, and quite lost their hearts.
 And daily new exactions are devised.

          Valmond and Musik confer with Camillo and Adrianna.
                   Beauchance and Lucinda embrace.

Beauchance. O Lucinda!

Lucinda. My husband!

Beauchance. If this be not a dream I see and hear!
 My wife, my queen, my life!
 How like a winter hath my absence been
 From thee.

Lucinda. My dearest husband!
> In this dull world, thy absence is as a death.
> Henceforth, nothing can dissolve us.

Beauchance. Ah dearest. First there is the Neapolitan
> Prince.

Lucinda. I will fasten on this sleeve of thine.

Beauchance. (*Embracing Lucinda.*) I have more care to
> stay than will to go.

Camillo. (*To Valmond.*) So that from point to point now
> have you heard
> The fundamental reasons of this war,
> Whose great decision hath much blood let forth
> And more thirsts after.

Valmond. Holy seems the quarrel
> Upon your grace's part; black and fearful
> On the oppose.

Camillo. Then you perceive the body of our kingdom
> How foul it is; what rank diseases grow,
> And with what danger, in the heart of it.

Adrianna. Make your own purpose, Duke, how in my
> strength
> You please. For you, whose virtue doth this instant
> So much commend itself, you shall be ours:
> Natures of such deep trust we shall much need.

Exit all but Valmond and Katrina.

Katrina. Our common theme now is death of fathers.

Valmond. I grieve to hear what torments you endured.

Katrina. I could weep o'er my brother's death anew.

Valmond. You will be revenged.

Katrina. And remembrance of my father never approaches
my heart but the tyranny of my sorrows, raining tears
of lamentation, takes all livelihood from my cheeks.
Grief hath changed me since you saw me last
And careful hours with time's deformed hand
Have written strange defeatures in my face.

Valmond. As you were when first your eye I eyed,
Such seems your beauty still.

Katrina. Humbly, I thank your grace for this high
courtesy.

Valmond. I must leave you within these two hours.
The leisure and the fearful time
Cuts off the interchange of sweet discourse.
For my part, I'll not trouble thee with words.
I have too few to take my leave of you,
When the tongue's office should be prodigal.

Katrina. Once more our minutes hasten to their end.

Valmond. This must my comfort be,
That sun that warms you here shall shine on me;
And those his golden beams to you here lent
Shall point on me.

Katrina. Here I will remain till thou return.

Valmond. If I am never to return, Princess,
Thou shalt live in this fair world behind,
Honour'd, beloved—

Katrina. O, confound the rest!

Valmond. I prithee now, hear me, sweet Katrina:
The web of our life is of a mingled yarn,
Good and ill together.
This world is not for aye, nor 'tis not strange
That even our loves should with our fortunes change;
For 'tis a question left us yet to prove,
Whether love lead fortune, or else fortune love.

And hitherto doth love on fortune tend.
Despite of all that I have thought or said,
As I do understand now,
Our wills and fates do so contrary run
That our devices still are overthrown;
Our thoughts are ours, their ends none of our own.
           (*beat*)
We must obey the time.

Katrina. O think'st thou we shall ever meet again?

Valmond. I doubt it not; and all these woes shall serve
For sweet discourses in our time to come. Farewell.

Katrina. Once more, adieu: be valiant, and speed well!

Exit severally. Blackout.

ACT IV

Scene 2

Central Sicily. The countryside. Before Valmond's tent.
Valmond, Camillo, Musik, Beauchance, and Captains.

Musik. The day begins to break, and night is fled,
  Whose pitchy mantle over-veil'd the earth.

Valmond. Send discoverers forth
  To know the numbers of our enemies.

Musik. We have sent forth already.

Enter first Captain.

First Captain. Royal commanders, be in readiness:
  West of this forest, scarcely off a mile,
  In goodly form comes on the enemy;
  And, by the ground they hide, I judge their number
  Upon or near the rate of thirty thousand.

Valmond. The question then standeth thus;
  Whether our present twenty thousand
  May hold up head.
  My brave and gentle knights, give me your thoughts:
  Think you not that the powers we bear with us
  Will cut their passage through the force of Naples,
  Doing the execution and the act
  For which we have in head assembled them?
  I pray you all,
  Speak plainly your opinions of our hopes.

Musik. In cases of defence 'tis best to weigh
  The enemy more mighty than he seems:
  So the proportions of defence are fill'd.

Camillo. With our small conjunction we should on,
    Then we shall shake off our slavish yoke,
    Imp out my drooping country's broken wing,
    Redeem from broking pawn the blemish'd crown,
    Wipe off the dust that hides our sceptre's gilt
    And make high majesty look like itself.

Beauchance. How much unlook'd for is this expedition!

Musik. By how much unexpected, by so much
    We must awake endeavor for defence;
    For courage mounteth with occasion:
    Let them be welcome then: we are prepared.
    We doubt not of a fair and lucky war.

Beauchance. (*Aside.*) I may not evermore behold my
        lady's face.
                (*To Valmond.*)
    My judgment is, we should not step too far
    Till we had assistance by the hand,
    For in a theme so bloody-faced as this,
    Conjecture, expectation and surmise
    Of aids incertain should not be admitted.
    My mind misgives
    Some consequence yet hanging in the stars.

Valmond. That's your superstition, my chevalier.

Beauchance. Then God's will be done.

Valmond. Now you would deliver
    Our puissance into the hand of God; but
    Men at some time are masters of their fates.

Musik. Count, 'tis true that we are in great danger;
    The greater therefore should our courage be.
    Valour's show and valour's worth divide
    In storms of fortune; then the thing of courage
    As roused with rage with rage doth sympathize,
    And with an accent tuned in selfsame key
    Retorts to chiding fortune.

       In the reproof of chance
       Lies the true proof of men.

Beauchance.   O, that a man might know
       The end of the day's business ere it come!

Musik.   It sufficeth that the day will end,
       And then the end is known.
       That we shall die, we know; 'tis but the time
       And drawing days out, that men stand upon.
       Why, courage then! what cannot be avoided
       'Twere childish weakness to lament or fear.

Valmond.   The spirit of my father grows strong in me;
       Methinks I hear him now: when I was young,
       I do remember how my father said,
       "Be great in act, as you have been in thought;
       Let not the world see fear and sad distrust
       Govern the motion of a royal eye:
       Be stirring as the time; be fire with fire;
       Threaten the threatener and outface the brow
       Of bragging horror: so shall inferior eyes,
       That borrow their behaviors from the great,
       Grow great by your example and put on
       The dauntless spirit of resolution.
       Show boldness and aspiring confidence."

Musik.   Were none more wise, my lord, than thy father.

Valmond.   (*To Beauchance.*) Cousin, go draw our
       puissance together.

              Blackout.

ACT IV

Scene 3

*Central Sicily. The countryside. Cosimo, Tertius, and
their force.*

Cosimo. The sun will not be seen today;
    The sky doth frown and lour upon our army.
    I would these dewy tears were from the ground.

Tertius. Young Duke Valmond doth join with Sicily;
    And, impatient of your just demands,
    Hath put himself in arms: the adverse winds,
    Whose leisure I have stay'd, have given him time
    To land his legions all as soon as I;
    His marches are expedient to this town,
    His forces strong, his soldiers confident.
    The interruption of their churlish drums
    Cuts off more circumstance: they are at hand,
    To parley or to fight; therefore prepare.

Cosimo. Summon a parley; we will talk with him.

*Enter Valmond, Camillo, Musik and the Burgundian
and Sicilian forces.*

Musik. They stand, and would have parley.

Tertius and Musik come towards each other.

Tertius. Prince Cosimo by me requests
    A parley with the Duke of Burgundy!

Musik. High-stomach'd are they both, and full of ire.

Tertius. Yea, in very truth, my lord.

*Musik returns to Valmond; Tertius to Cosimo; Valmond
and company approach Cosimo and company.*

Cosimo. Young Duke, be pleased to tell your allies
          To pay that duty which they truly owe:
          And then
          With unhack'd swords and helmets all unbruised,
          We will bear home that lusty blood again
          Which here we came to spout, and leave in peace.
          Then tell us, shall this country call us lord,
          In that behalf which we have challenged it?
          Or shall we give the signal to our rage
          And stalk in blood to our possession?

Valmond. We will not budge, and we will nothing pay.
          These flags of Sicily, that are advanced here
          Before the eye and prospect of your force,
          Have hither march'd to your endamagement.
          I will have my revenge ere I depart.

Cosimo. This apish and unmannerly approach,
          This harness'd masque and unadvised revel,
          This unhair'd sauciness and boyish troops,
          Our force doth smile at; and is well prepared
          To whip this dwarfish war, these pigmy arms,
          From out the circle of this territory.
          If Sicily would the peace,
          You must buy that peace
          With full accord to all our just demands.
          Call my sovereign yours;
          And do him homage as obedient subjects;
          And I'll withdraw me and my bloody power.

Valmond. This is not well, deliver up the crown;
          See'st thou? Within a ken our army lies,
          Upon mine honour, all too confident
          To give admittance to a thought of fear.
          What say you to it? will you unknit
          This churlish knot of all-abhorred war?

Cosimo. Burgundy, take mercy
    On the poor souls for whom this hungry war
    Opens his vasty jaws; and on your head
    Turning the widows' tears, the orphans' cries,
    The dead men's blood, the pining maidens' groans,
    For husbands, fathers and betrothed lovers,
    That shall be swallow'd in this controversy.

Valmond. God forgive the sin of all those souls
    That to their everlasting residence,
    Before the dew of evening, shall fleet,
    In dreadful trial of this kingdom's queen!

Cosimo. Dare ye come forth and meet us in the field?
    Have I not here the best cards for the game,
    To win this easy match play'd for a crown?
    And shall I now give o'er the yielded set?
    No, no, on my soul, it never shall be said.

Valmond. Know thou, that once we have begun to strike,
    We'll never leave till we have hewn thee down,
    And I shall sweep to my revenge.

Cosimo. Our battle is more full of names than yours,
    Our men more perfect in the use of arms.

Valmond. Our armour all as strong, our cause the best.

Cosimo. Then you shall open
    The purple testament of bleeding war.

Valmond. Then prepare.

Cosimo. By heaven!
    My blood hath been too cold and temperate,
    Unapt to stir at these indignities;
    You tread upon my patience: but be sure
    I will from henceforth rather be myself,
    Mighty and to be fear'd, than my condition;
    Which hath been smooth as oil, soft as young down,

And therefore lost that title of respect
Which the proud soul ne'er pays but to the proud.

Valmond. Prince, I grant thee bloody, avaricious, false,
deceitful, sudden, malicious.
But thou doth lack the king-becoming graces,
As justice, verity, temperance, stableness,
Bounty, perseverance, mercy, lowliness,
Devotion, patience, courage, fortitude.

Cosimo. Break off the parley; for scarce I can refrain
The execution of my big-swoln heart
Upon this paltry, insolent fellow.
All the budding honours on thy crest
I'll crop, to make a garland for my head.

Valmond. Naples, thou shalt rue this hour within the hour.

Exit severally. Blackout.

ACT IV

Scene 4

Central Sicily. Field of battle in countryside. Valmond,
Camillo, Musik, Beauchance, Perfumo, Rinaldo, Captains,
and Soldiers.

Valmond. Guy de Beauchance, Count of Provence,
    The general of our horse thou art; and we,
    Great in our hope, lay our best love and credence
    Upon thy promising fortune.

Beauchance. Sir, it is
    A charge too heavy for my strength, but yet
    We'll strive to bear it for your worthy sake
    To the extreme edge of hazard.

Drums approach.

Valmond. I hear their drums: let's set our men in order,
    And issue forth and bid them battle straight.
    Valiant soldiers of Sicily
    And my loyal subjects of Burgundy,
    When the blast of war blows in our ears,
    Then imitate the action of the tiger;
    Stiffen the sinews, summon up the blood,
    Disguise fair nature with hard-favour'd rage;
    Then lend the eye a terrible aspect;
    Let it pry through the portage of the head
    Like the brass cannon; let the brow o'erwhelm it;
    Now set the teeth and stretch the nostril wide,
    Hold hard the breath and bend up every spirit
    To his full height. Good yeomen, show us here
    The mettle of your pasture; let us swear
    That you are worth your breeding; which I doubt not;
    For there is none of you so mean and base,
    That hath not noble lustre in your eyes.

I see you stand like greyhounds in the slips,
Straining upon the start. The game's afoot:
Follow your spirit. And now no more ado,
But gather we our forces out of hand
And set upon our boasting enemy.
Therefore, to arms!

Rinaldo. Zounds! I am burn'd up with inflaming wrath
That nothing can allay, nothing but blood,
The blood, and dearest-valued blood, of Naples.

Valmond. Then go thou forth.
Now bind my brows with iron; and approach
The ragged'st hour that time and spite dare bring.
Let us march cheerly on, courageous friends,
To reap the harvest of perpetual peace
By this one bloody trial of sharp war.

Alarums near and far. Exit all, charging. Skirmishes.
Flourish. Enter Cosimo, Tertius, Captains.

Tertius. Where have they this mettle? If they march along
Unfought withal, but I will sell my dukedom.

Cosimo. Up my lords, and, with spirit of honor edged
More sharper than your swords, hie to the field.
Great dukes and barons, captains, lords and knights,
For your great seats now quit you of great shames.
Rush on this host, as doth the melted snow
Upon the valleys, whose low vassal seat
The Alps doth spit and void his rheum upon:
Go down upon them, you have power enough,
And bring Burgundy our prisoner.
All form is formless, order orderless,
Save what to Sicily is opposite.

Alarums. Exit Neapolitans, retreating. Skirmishes.
Enter Rinaldo, fighting off two Neapolitan Soldiers; one
wounds him then both flee. Rinaldo bleeds.

Rinaldo. If I be killed, but one dead that was willing
　　　To be so: by my troth, I care not; a man
　　　Can die but once: we owe God a death:
　　　I'll ne'er bear a base mind: an't be my destiny.

Enter Perfumo.

Perfumo. Signior Rinaldo, worthy sir, thou bleed'st;
　　　Thy exercise hath been too violent for
　　　A second course of fight.

Rinaldo. Praise me not, Signior Perfumo;
　　　My work hath yet not warm'd me: fare you well:
　　　The blood I drop is rather physical
　　　Than dangerous to me.

Perfumo. Now the fair goddess, Fortune,
　　　Fall deep in love with thee; and her great charms
　　　Misguide thy opposers' swords!
　　　As good to die and go, as die and stay.

Exit Perfumo.

Rinaldo. Fate, show thy force: ourselves we do not owe;
　　　What is decreed must be, and be this so.
　　　Let time shape, and there an end.

*Exit. Alarums. Skirmishes. Retreat. Enter two Sicilian
Captains.*

First Sicilian Captain. Blood hath bought blood and blows
　　　have answered blows;
　　　Strength match'd with strength, and power confronted
　　　power:
　　　Both are alike.

Second Sicilian Captain. The disorder's such as war were
　　　hoodwink'd.

Enter Beauchance and Soldiers.

Beauchance. This battle fares like to the morning's war,
    When dying clouds contend with growing light,
    Now sways it this way, like a mighty sea
    Forced by the tide to combat with the wind;
    Now one the better, then another best;
    Sometime the flood prevails, and then the wind;
    Now one the better, then another best;
    Both tugging to be victors, breast to breast,
    Yet neither conqueror nor conquered:
    So is the equal poise of this fell war.

           Flourish. Enter Valmond.

Valmond. Stand, stand! We have the advantage of the
       ground.
    We must take the current when it serves
    Or lose our ventures.

Beauchance. I do beseech you, by the vows
    We have made to endure friends, that you directly
    Set me against Cosimo and his guard;
    And that you not delay the present, but,
    Filling the air with swords advanced and darts,
    We prove this very hour.

Valmond. Take your choice of those
    That best can aid your action.

Beauchance. Those are they
    That most are willing. So many so minded,
    Wave thus, to express his disposition, and follow.

    Flourish. Exit all. Alarums. Skirmishes. Enter
   Neapolitan Soldiers in retreat, cross over, and exit,
      followed by two Neapolitan Captains.

First Neapolitan Captain. How appears the fight?

Second Neapolitan Captain. On our side like the token'd
       pestilence,
    Where death is sure.

First Neapolitan Captain. We hear this fearful tempest
      sing,
  Yet seek no shelter to avoid the storm.

Second Neapolitan Captain. The noise is round about us.

First Neapolitan Captain. Let us from it.

Second Neapolitan Captain. Nay, what hope have we in
      hiding us? This way
  The French must or the Sicilians slay us.

First Neapolitan Captain. I have lost my hopes.

Second Neapolitan Captain. Perchance even there where I
      did find my doubts.

         Alarums. Enter Cosimo, cursing.

Cosimo. All the contagion of the south light on you,
  You shames! you herd of—how have you run
  From slaves that apes would beat! Pluto and hell!
  All hurt behind; backs red, and faces pale
  With flight and agued fear! mend and charge home,
  Or, by the fires of heaven, I'll leave the foe
  And make my wars on you: look to't: come on;
  If you'll stand fast, we'll beat them to their wives,
  As they us to our trenches followed.

         Enter Third Neapolitan Captain.

Third Neapolitan Captain. I ran from the river, my noble
      lord;
  Where hateful death put on his ugliest mask
  To fright our party.

Cosimo. This sickness doth infect
  The very life-blood of our enterprise.
  O war, thou son of hell,
  Whom angry heavens do make their minister,
  Throw in the frozen bosoms of our part

Hot coals of vengeance! Let no soldier fly.
He that is truly dedicate to war
Hath no self-love, nor he that loves himself
Hath not essentially but by circumstance
The name of valour.
Today how many would have given their honours
To have saved their carcasses! took heel to do't,
And yet died too! I never saw an action of such shame;
Experience, manhood, honour, ne'er before
Did violate so itself.
Shame and eternal shame, nothing but shame!
Let us die in honour: once more back again.
Disorder, that hath spoil'd us, friend us now!
Let us on heaps go offer up our lives.

First Neapolitan Captain. The loyalty well held to fools
      does make
Our faith mere folly.

Third Neapolitan Captain. Yet he that can endure
      To follow with allegiance a fall'n lord
      Does conquer him that did his master conquer
      And earns a place i' the story.

Exit Neapolitan Captains.

Cosimo. There's some ill planet reigns:
      A greater power than we can contradict
      Hath thwarted our intents.
      I must be patient till the heavens look
      With an aspect more favorable.

*Alarums. Exit Cosimo. Skirmishes. Alarums. Enter
Cambio and Neapolitan Soldiers.*

Cambio. My stars shine darkly over me: the malignancy of
      my fate might perhaps distemper yours; therefore I
      shall crave of you your leave that I may bear my evils
      alone.

First Neapolitan Soldier. Have not to do with him, beware
   of him;
  Sin, death, and hell have set their marks on him,
  And all their ministers attend on him.

    Exit Neapolitan Soldiers.

Cambio. I must go and meet with danger
  Or it will seek me in another place.

    Exit Cambio. Enter Perfumo.

Perfumo. I am as hot as molten lead. God keep lead out of
   me!

    Enter Musik.

Musik. What, stand'st thou idle here? Lend me thy sword:
  Many a nobleman lies stark and stiff
  Whose deaths are yet unrevenged.

Perfumo. I prithee, give me leave to breathe awhile.
  I would 'twere bed-time, and all well.

Musik. What, is it a time to jest and dally now?
  Thou owest God a death.
  Say thy prayers, and farewell.

    Alarums. Exit Musik.

Perfumo. 'Tis not due yet; I would be loath to pay him
   before his day.
  A sword and boar-spear in my hand;
  We'll have a swashing and a martial outside,
  As many other mannish cowards have
  That do outface it with their semblances.

    Re-enter Cambio.

Cambio. Avaunt, thou hateful villain, get thee gone!

Perfumo. I am no villain. Stand back, stand back, I say;
  By heaven, I think my sword's as sharp as yours:
  I would not have you, sir, forget yourself,
  Nor tempt the danger of my true defence.

Cambio. Out, dunghill! darest thou brave a nobleman?

Perfumo. Not for my life: but yet I dare defend
  My innocent life against an emperor.

*They fight. Cambio is disarmed and falls. Perfumo backs
    away and exits.*

Cambio. By the elements,
  If e'er again I meet him beard to beard,
  He's mine, or I am his: where
  I thought to crush him in an equal force,
  True sword to sword, I'll potch at him some way
  Or wrath or craft may get him.
  Forspent with toil, as runners with a race,
  I lay me down a little while to breathe;
  For strokes received, and many blows repaid,
  Have robb'd my strong-knit sinews of their strength,
  And spite of spite needs must I rest awhile.
  Alas. I am a wretch whom nature is asham'd
  Almost t' acknowledge hers. I hate myself
  For hateful deeds committed by myself.
  O conscience, how dost thou afflict me!
  I'll not meddle with it: it makes a man a coward.

Enter Valmond from behind. He listens.

Cambio. (*Cont'd.*) I know all the particulars of vice:
  There's no bottom to my voluptuousness;
  I have served the lust of my mistress' heart, and did the
  act of darkness with her; swore as many oaths as I
  spake words, and broke them in the sweet face of
  heaven: slept in the contriving of lust, and waked to do
  it: wine loved I deeply, dice dearly: bloody of hand; hog
  in sloth, fox in stealth, wolf in greediness, dog in
  madness, lion in prey.

The heaviness and guilt within my bosom
Takes off my manhood: I have belied a lady,
The princess of this country, and the air on't
Revengingly enfeebles me; or could this carl,
A very drudge of nature's, have subdued me
In my profession?

Cambio rises and retrieves his sword. Valmond steps
forward.

Valmond. Beshrew my heart, accursed miscreant;
I know thee well: a serviceable villain.
You never spoke what did become you less
Than this.
Thou'rt damn'd as black—nay, nothing is so black;
Thou art more deep damn'd than Prince Lucifer:
There is not yet so ugly a fiend of hell
As thou shalt be.

Cambio. Stand by, or I shall gall you, Burgundy.

Valmond. Thou wert better gall the devil, coward:
I'll so maul you and your toasting-iron,
That you shall think the devil is come from hell.
And so, have at thee.

They fight. Valmond mortally stabs Cambio. He falls.

Cambio. My mangled body doth show my sick heart.
My soul is heavy, and I fain would sleep.
Here will I set up my everlasting rest,
And shake the yoke of inauspicious stars
From this world-wearied flesh.
Tell the princess I beg her forgiveness.
O God and heaven, forgive me my sins.

Cambio dies. Exit Valmond. Re-enter Perfumo. He
approaches the body, kicks it, and picks up the sword.

Perfumo. A heavy reckoning for you, sir. But the comfort
is, you shall be called to no more payments, fear no

more tavern-bills; which are often the sadness of
parting, as the procuring of mirth: you come in faint for
want of meat, depart reeling with too much drink; sorry
that you have paid too much, and sorry that you are
paid too much; purse and brain both empty; the brain
the heavier for being too light, the purse too light, being
drawn of heaviness: of this contradiction you shall now
be quit. Come you along with me.

Exit Perfumo, dragging the dead body.

ACT IV

Scene 5

*Central Sicily. The field of battle. Cosimo and Tertius
survey the field.*

Tertius. My liege: why looks your grace so pale?

Cosimo. Have I not reason to look pale and dead?
    All my followers to the eager foe
    Turn back and fly, like ships before the wind
    Or lambs pursued by hunger-starved wolves.
    Shame and confusion! all is on the rout.

        Enter three Neapolitan Captains.

First Neapolitan Captain. Our hap is loss, our hope but
       sad despair;
    Our ranks are broke, and ruin follows us.

Second Neapolitan Captain. Our sons lie scattered on the
       bleeding ground;
    Many a widow's husband grovelling lies,
    Coldly embracing the discolour'd earth;
    And victory, with little loss, doth play
    Upon the dancing banners of Valmond.

Cosimo. All is confounded, all!
    Reproach and everlasting shame
    Sits mocking in our plumes.

Tertius. We bodged again; as I have seen a swan
    With bootless labour swim against the tide
    And spend her strength with over-matching waves.

        Alarums.

Second Neapolitan Captain.   Ah, hark! the fatal followers
       do pursue;
     What counsel give you? whither shall we fly?

Cosimo.   I am faint and cannot fly their fury:
     Were I strong, I would not shun their fury.
     Cease your ire, you angry stars of heaven!
     My good stars, that were my former guides,
     Have empty left their orbs, and shot their fires
     Into the abysm of hell.

Tertius.   When Fortune in her shift and change of mood
     Spurns down her late beloved, all his dependants
     Which labour'd after him to the mountain's top
     Even on their knees and hands, let him slip down,
     Not one accompanying his declining foot.

Third Neapolitan Captain.   Not being Fortune, he's but
       Fortune's knave,
     A minister of her will.

       Exit all but Cosimo. He kneels on the ground.

Cosimo.   From the full meridian of my glory,
     I haste now to my setting: I shall fall
     Like a bright exhalation in the evening,
     And no man see me more.
     O God! Methinks it were a happy life,
     To be no better than a homely swain;
     To sit upon a hill,
     To carve out dials quaintly, point by point,
     Thereby to see the minutes how they run,
     How many make the hour full complete;
     How many hours bring about the day;
     How many days will finish up the year;
     How many years a mortal man may live.
     Some one, give me a bowl of wine:
     I have not that alacrity of spirit,
     Nor cheer of mind, that I was wont to have.

           Blackout.

ACT IV

Scene 6

Central Sicily. Camp of Valmond's forces. Valmond,
Camillo, Pierre, Musik, Perfumo, and Soldier.

Pierre. The valiant Signior Rinaldo:
    When he perceived me shrink and on my knee,
    His bloody sword he brandish'd over me,
    And, like a hungry lion, did commence
    Rough deeds of rage and stern impatience;
    But when my angry guardant stood alone,
    Suddenly made him from my side to start
    Into the clustering battle, and there died.
           (*To Perfumo.*)
    I am sorry I should force you to believe
    That which I would to God I had not seen;
    But these mine eyes saw him in bloody state.

        Soldiers carry in body of Rinaldo.

Musik. See how the blood is settled in his face.
    Oft have I seen a timely-parted ghost,
    Of ashy semblance, meagre, pale and bloodless,
    Being all descended to the labouring heart;
    Which the heart there cools and ne'er returneth
    To blush and beautify the cheek again.
    But see, his face is black and full of blood,
    His eye-balls further out than when he lived,
    Staring full ghastly like a strangled man;
    His hair uprear'd, his nostrils stretched with
        struggling;
    His hands abroad display'd, as one that grasp'd
    And tugg'd for life and was by strength subdued.

Perfumo. Thou antic death, which laugh'st us here to
    scorn.

So dear I loved the man, that I must weep.
I took him for the plainest harmless creature
That breathed upon this earth a Christian.
Shall I abide in this dull world?

Pierre. Well, peace be with him that hath made us heavy!

Perfumo. Ay, but to die, and go we know not where;
To lie in cold obstruction and to rot;
This sensible warm motion to become
A kneaded clod; and the delighted spirit
To bathe in fiery floods, or to reside
In thrilling region of thick-ribbed ice;
To be imprison'd in the viewless winds,
And blown with restless violence round about
The pendent world; or to be worse than worst
Of those that lawless and incertain thought
Imagine howling: 'tis too horrible!
The weariest and most loathed worldly life
That age, ache, penury and imprisonment
Can lay on nature is a paradise
To what we fear of death.

Musik. All is said:
His tongue is now a stringless instrument;
Words, life, and all.

*Soldiers carry out body of Rinaldo; Perfumo follows.
Enter Cosimo, led by Soldiers and placed before
Valmond etc.*

Valmond. Prince Cosimo, in this fair kingdom
Thou hast under-wrought the lawful king,
Cut off the sequence of posterity,
And done a rape
Upon the maiden virtue of the crown.

Cosimo. Duke of Burgundy, I am thy prisoner;
Thus far thy fortune keeps an upward course,
And thou art graced with wreaths of victory.
Let those who are in favour with their stars

Of public honour and proud titles boast.
I here resign my government to thee,
For thou art fortunate in all thy deeds.

Valmond. We bear our fortunes in our own strong arms.
See what now thou art:
For one being sued to, one that humbly sues;
For one that scorn'd at me, now scorn'd of me;
For one being fear'd of all, now fearing one;
For one commanding all, obey'd of none.
Thus hath the course of justice wheel'd about.

Cosimo. Paltry fellow; you tread upon my patience.

Valmond. I warn thee, Prince: be humble to us.
One fire drives out one fire; one nail, one nail;
Rights by rights falter, strengths by strengths do fail.
'Tis certain, greatness, once fall'n out with fortune,
Must fall out with men too.

Cosimo. We trifle time: I pray thee, pursue sentence.

Valmond. Cheque thy contempt: obey our will.
I will have my revenge, ere we depart.

Cosimo. Sir, spare me your threats.

Valmond. Hear this:
Your ransom must proportion the losses we have
borne, the subjects we have lost. For our losses, your
exchequer is too poor; for the effusion of our blood,
the muster of your kingdom too faint a number; and
for our disgrace, your own person, kneeling at our feet,
but a weak and worthless satisfaction. Hear your
sentence.

Cosimo. The worst is worldly loss thou canst unfold.
Cry woe, destruction, ruin and decay:
The worst is death, and death will have his day.

Musik. Such hollow men, like horses hot at hand,
　　Make gallant show and promise of their mettle;
　　But when they should endure the bloody spur,
　　They fall their crests.

Valmond. (*Growing impatient.*) Before we do condemn
　　thee, Prince of Naples, you shall repent your folly, see
　　your weakness, and admire our sufferance.

Cosimo. My imperial tongue is stern and rough,
　　Used to command, untaught to plead for favour.
　　No, rather let my head
　　Stoop to the block than these knees bow to any.

Valmond. Very well then; thou shalt die.

Cosimo. What!

Valmond. Death! Drawn on with torture.

Cosimo. A heavy sentence, my lord!
　　And all unlook'd for from your highness' mouth!

Valmond. After our sentence, plaining comes too late.

Cosimo. You shall have ransom. What ransom must I
　　　　pay?
　　I beg of you. 'Tis no time to jest.

Valmond. Firm and irrevocable is my doom.

Cosimo. I do repent me! I do repent me!
　　Draw near our God in being merciful:
　　Sweet mercy is nobility's true badge.
　　My ransom will soon be levied!

Valmond. See him deliver'd over to execution.

Exit Valmond.

Beauchance. (*Aside to all but Cosimo.*) 'Tis but his jesting
　　spirit. I think.

Exit Beauchance, Musik, and Camillo.

Cosimo. Hold! I do repent me from my very soul!
     Be not so rash; take ransom, let me live!

Cosimo watches all exit.

Cosimo. (*Cont'd.*) The sands are number'd that make up
         my life.
     Lo, now my glory smear'd in dust and blood!
     My parks, my walks, my manors that I had,
     Even now forsake me, and of all my lands
     Is nothing left me but my body's length.
     Why, what is pomp, rule, reign, but earth and dust?
     Would I were dead! if God's good will were so;
     For what is in this world but grief and woe.
     I see that Time's the king of men,
     He's both their parent, and he is their grave,
     And gives them what he will, not what they crave.
     O, hear me then, injurious, shifting Time!
     Mis-shapen Time, copesmate of ugly Night,
     Swift subtle post, carrier of grisly care,
     Eater of youth, false slave to false delight,
     Base watch of woes, sin's pack-horse, virtue's snare;
     Thou nursest all and murder'st all that are.
     I wasted time, and now doth time waste me.
     The end crowns all.

First Soldier. Thus the whirligig of time brings in his
     revenges.

Second Soldier. All unavoided is the doom of destiny.

Blackout.

ACT V

Scene 1

Palermo. Before the royal palace. Flourish. Cornets.
Townspeople watch and cheer entering Soldiers. Katrina,
Lucinda, Sophia, and Adrianna watch from palace steps.

First Townsman. Like a troop of jolly huntsmen, come
　　Our lusty soldiers, all with purpled hands,
　　Dyed in the dying slaughter of their foes.

Second Townsman. Beat loud the tabourines, let the
　　　trumpets blow,
　　That these great soldiers may their welcome know.

First Townsman. Have you seen the young Duke of
　　Burgundy?

Second Townsman. All tongues speak of him.

Third Townsman. They do report he is a creature such
　　As, to seek through the regions of the earth
　　For one his like, there would be something failing
　　In him that should compare: most praised, most loved,
　　A sample to the youngest, to the more mature
　　A glass that feated them.

Second Townsman. 'Tis said the bleared sights
　　Are spectacled to see him: your prattling nurse
　　Into a rapture lets her baby cry
　　While she chats him: the kitchen malkin pins
　　Her richest lockram 'bout her reechy neck,
　　Clambering the walls to eye him.

Third Townsman. Stalls, bulks, windows,
　　Are smother'd up, leads fill'd, and ridges horsed
　　With variable complexions, all agreeing
　　In earnestness to see him.

Second Townsman. Seld-shown flamens
     Do press among the popular throngs and puff
     To win a vulgar station: or veil'd dames
     Commit the war of white and damask in
     Their nicely-gawded cheeks.

First Townsman. Wait! Now I see the duke, great
        Burgundy,
     Mounted upon a hot and fiery steed,
     With slow but stately pace.
     You would think the very windows do speak,
     So many greedy looks of young and old
     Through casements dart their desiring eyes
     Upon his visage.

Third Townsman. I do not think
     So fair an outward and such stuff within
     Endows a man but he:
     His looks are full of peaceful majesty,
     His head by nature framed to wear a crown,
     His hand to wield a sceptre, and himself
     Likely in time to bless a regal throne.
     He dismounts.

All. God save thee, Burgundy!
     Jesu preserve thee! welcome, Burgundy!

     Cornets. Enter Valmond, Camillo, Beauchance, Musik,
        Pierre, Captains, and Soldiers, all waving.

Katrina. (*Aside.*) If I may trust the flattering truth of
        sleep,
     My dreams presage some joyful news at hand:
     My bosom's lord sits lightly in his throne;
     And all this day an unaccustom'd spirit
     Lifts me above the ground with cheerful thoughts.

        All bow to Adrianna.

Adrianna. I multiply with one "We thank you"
     Many thousands moe that go before it.

Valmond. Please give your thanks to these soldiers.
        Unto these men do I in chief address
        The substance of my speech. I thank you all;
        For doughty-handed are you, and have fought
        Not as you served the cause, but as 't had been
        Each man's like mine; you have shown all Hectors.
        Enter the city, clip your wives, your friends,
        Tell them your feats; whilst they with joyful tears
        Wash the congealment from your wounds, and kiss
        The honour'd gashes whole.
        But yet, let's not forget Amadeo,
        The noble Prince of Sicily, late deceased.
        A braver soldier never couched lance,
        A gentler heart did never sway in court.
        I shall lack voice: the deeds of Amadeo
        Should not be utter'd feebly. It is held
        That valour is the chiefest virtue, and
        Most dignifies the haver: if it be,
        The man I speak of cannot in the world
        Be singly counterpoised.
        His face was as the heavens; and therein stuck
        A sun and moon, which kept their course, and lighted
        The little O, the earth.
        His voice was propertied
        As all the tuned spheres, and that to friends;
        But when he meant to quail and shake the orb,
        He was as rattling thunder. For his bounty,
        There was no winter in't; his delights
        Were dolphin-like; they show'd his back above
        The element they lived in; and the elements
        So mix'd in him that Nature might stand up
        And say to all the world "This was a man!"
        I honoured him, I loved him, and will weep
        My date of life out for his sweet life's loss.

Townspeople disperse. Exit Adrianna and attendants.
Beauchance and Lucinda exit together. Valmond joins
Katrina.

Katrina. Since I saw you last, there is a change upon you.

Valmond. Well, I know not
What counts harsh fortune casts upon my face.
But give me audience, good madam.
This I must say—

Katrina. Proceed.

Valmond. I would say—pray, pardon me, Princess.
(*Stumbling over his words, lifting the chain
that hangs around his neck.*)
I must say—that I know myself now;
And I feel within me a—

Katrina. O, ominous!

Valmond. Will you speak?

Katrina. Do you not know I am a woman? When I think,
I must speak. Sweet, say on.

Valmond. Time, force, and death
Do to this body what extremes it can,
The strong base and building of my love
Is as the very centre of the earth,
Drawing all things to it. My love is—

Katrina. Heavens! Thy love?

Valmond. Dearest one! Alas. I do love nothing in the
world so well as you.

Katrina. (*Touching the chain.*) I was about to protest I
loved you.

Valmond. And do it with all thy heart.

Katrina. I love you with so much of my heart that none is
left.

Valmond. Lest my liking might too sudden seem,
I would have salved it with a longer treatise.
Teach me, dear creature, how to think and speak.

Katrina. Say thou art mine, dear Valmond, and ever
     My love as it began shall so persevere.

Valmond. I love you more than words can wield the
          matter;
     Dearer than eye-sight, space, and liberty;
     Beyond what can be valued, rich or rare;
     No less than life, with grace, health, beauty, honour;
     A love that makes breath poor, and speech unable;
     Beyond all manner of so much I love you.

Katrina. When you speak, sweet, I'ld have you do it ever.

Valmond. Thou hast made my heart
     Too great for what contains it!

Katrina. This is the very ecstasy of love!

                    They embrace. Blackout.

ACT V

Scene 2

*Palermo. Inside the royal palace. Camillo, Valmond,
Lords, and Musik. Enter Morelli, under guard, and
Duchess.*

First Lord. Treasons capital, confess'd and proved
    Have overthrown him.

Second Lord. He was the covert'st sheltered traitor
    That ever lived.
    So smooth he daub'd his vice with show of virtue,
    That, his apparent open guilt omitted,
    He lived from all attainder of suspect;
    A recreant and most degenerate traitor.

First Lord. A common fiend, that's without faith or love;
    Too good to be so and too bad to live.

Enter Adrianna, attended.

Second Lord. Queen Adrianna,
    Very frankly he confess'd his treasons,
    Implored your highness' pardon and set forth
    A deep repentance.

First Lord. Morelli, Duke of Messina, brother to the
    worthy Lucentio, late King of Sicily, thou art here
    accused and arraigned of high treason.

Morelli. This is the state of man: today he puts forth
    The tender leaves of hopes; tomorrow blossoms,
    And bears his blushing honours thick upon him;
    The third day comes a frost, a killing frost,
    And, when he thinks, good easy man, full surely
    His greatness is a-ripening, nips his root,
    And then he falls, as I do.

Second Lord. Now does he feel his title
　　　Hang loose about him, like a giant robe
　　　Upon a dwarfish thief.

Morelli. Now I feel
　　　Of what coarse metal ye are moulded, envy:
　　　How eagerly ye follow my disgraces,
　　　As if it fed ye! and how sleek and wanton
　　　Ye appear in every thing may bring my ruin!
　　　Follow your envious courses, men of malice;
　　　No doubt, in time ye'll find your fit rewards.

Camillo. Thou art an enemy to peace;
　　　Wicked, pestiferous, and dissentious;
　　　And for thy treachery, what's more manifest?
　　　In that thou laid'st a trap to take the life
　　　Of Prince Amadeo?

Morelli. Were I chief lord of all this spacious world,
　　　I'ld give it to undo my deeds.

Adrianna. What shall I say to thee, traitor duke? thou
　　　　　cruel,
　　　Ingrateful, savage and inhuman creature!
　　　Thou that didst bear the key of all our counsels.
　　　Treason and murder ever kept together,
　　　As two yoke-devils sworn to either's purpose;
　　　But thou, 'gainst all proportion, didst bring in
　　　Wonder to wait on treason and on murder:
　　　And whatsoever cunning fiend it was
　　　That wrought upon thee so preposterously
　　　Hath got the voice in hell for excellence:
　　　He that temper'd thee bade thee stand up,
　　　Gave thee no instance why thou shouldst do treason,
　　　Unless to dub thee with the name of traitor.
　　　If that same demon that hath gull'd thee thus
　　　Should with his lion gait walk the whole world,
　　　He might return to vasty Tartar back,
　　　And tell the legions "I can never win
　　　A soul so easy as that Sicilian's."

O, how hast thou with jealousy infected
The sweetness of affiance! Show men dutiful?
Why, so didst thou: seem they grave and learned?
Why, so didst thou: come they of noble family?
Why, so didst thou: seem they religious?
Why, so didst thou:
Such and so finely bolted didst thou seem:
And thus thy fall hath left a kind of blot,
To mark the full-fraught man and best indued
With some suspicion.
This revolt of thine, methinks, is like
Another fall of man.

Morelli. Yea, mark my fall, and that that ruined me.
Brother, I charge thee, fling away ambition:
By that sin fell the angels; how can man, then,
The image of his Maker, hope to win by it?
Vain pomp and glory of this world, I hate ye:
I feel my heart new open'd. Your highness,
Pardon me my wrongs and by my soul I swear
I never more will break an oath with thee.

First Lord. Let them not live to taste this land's increase
That would with treason wound this fair land's peace!

Duchess. On my knees I beg your highness:
Have mercy on us; pardon the duke.

Adrianna. Though with thy high wrongs I am struck to the
quick,
Yet with my nobler reason 'gainst my fury
Do I take part. For thy daughter's sake,
Thou shalt not die.
Thy lands and all things that thou dost call thine
Worth seizure do we seize into our hands;
Turn thou no more to seek a living in our territory.

Morelli. Queen, wouldst thou have us go and beg our
food?

Adrianna. Good sooth, I care not. Get you from our court;
     Dispatch you with your utmost haste;
     If thou linger
     Longer than swiftest expedition
     Will give thee time to leave our royal court,
     By heaven! my wrath shall far exceed the love
     I ever bore thy daughter or thy wife.
     Within these two days if that thou be'st found
     Within this kingdom thou diest for it.
     Thou art banished, banished on pain of death.

Morelli. But, my queen—

Adrianna. Be gone! I will not hear thy vain excuse;
     Avaunt, thou hateful villain, get thee gone.
     Both thee and thy wife.

Morelli. Then thus I turn me from my country's light.
     So, farewell, Sicily; sweet soil, adieu.

        Exit Morelli, under guard, and Duchess.

Adrianna. Thus have we swept villainy from our seat
     And made our footstool of security.
     Publish we this peace
     To all our subjects, and seal it with feasts.
     Duke Valmond, our brother Camillo has
     Made me acquainted with a weighty cause
     Of love between my daughter and yourself:
     And for the excellence I know of you
     And for the love you beareth to Katrina
     And she to you, I am content to have
     You match'd. Bring in our daughter.

        Enter Katrina, Lucinda, and Beauchance.

Adrianna. See where she comes, apparell'd like the spring,
     Graces her subjects, and her thoughts the king
     Of every virtue gives renown to men!

Camillo. Her face the book of praises, where is read
     Nothing but curious pleasures, as from thence

        Sorrow were ever razed and testy wrath
        Could never be her mild companion.

Adrianna. At her conception nature this dowry gave;
        The senate-house of planets all did sit
        To knit her in their best perfections.

Musik. By her election may be truly read
        What kind of man young Valmond is;
        Princess Katrina's own price
        Proclaims how she esteems him and his virtue.

Beauchance. (*To Katrina.*) Look upon him, love him, he
        worships you.

Adrianna. Never gazed the moon
        Upon the water as he stands and reads
        As 'twere my daughter's eyes; and, to be plain,
        I think there is not half a kiss to choose
        Who loves another best.
                (*To Valmond.*)
        I give you here a half of mine own life,
        Or that for which I live.

Valmond. (*To Adrianna.*) You may be sure
        I count myself in nothing else so happy.
                (*To Katrina.*)
        I would not wish
        Any companion in the world but you,
        Nor can imagination form a shape,
        Besides yourself, to like of.

Katrina. For myself alone
        I would not be ambitious in my wish,
        To wish myself much better; yet, for you
        I would be trebled twenty times myself;
        A thousand times more fair, ten thousand times more
            rich;
        That only to stand high in your account,
        I might in virtue, beauties, livings, friends,
        Exceed account; my gentle spirit

Commits itself to yours;
Myself and what is mine to you and yours
Is now converted.

Valmond. And, as my fortune ripens with thy love,
It shall be still thy true love's recompense.

Katrina. Dearest Valmond, by the roses of the spring,
By maidhood, honour, truth and every thing,
I love thee so, that, maugre all my pride,
Nor wit nor reason can my passion hide.

Valmond. Thou art mine own self's better part,
Mine eye's clear eye, my dear heart's dearer heart,
My food, my fortune and my sweet hope's aim,
My sole earth's heaven and my heaven's claim.
My heart this covenant makes, my hand thus seals it.
Love for thy love and hand for hand I give.
Two bosoms interchained with an oath;
So then two bosoms and a single troth.

Katrina. Love teacheth us that thou and I am one:
That my heart unto yours is knit
So that but one heart we can make of it.

Adrianna. Now all the blessings
Of a glad mother comfort thee about!
Combine your hearts in one, our realms in one!
As man and wife, being two, are one in love,
So be there 'twixt our kingdoms such a spousal,
That never may ill office, or fell jealousy,
Which troubles oft the bed of blessed marriage,
Thrust in between the paction of these kingdoms,
To make divorce of their incorporate league.
All is whole;
To solemnize this day the glorious sun
Stays in his course and plays the alchemist,
Turning with splendor of his precious eye
The meagre cloddy earth to glittering gold:
The yearly course that brings this day about
Shall never see it but a holiday.

And now what rests but that we spend the time
With stately triumphs, mirthful comic shows,
Such as befits the pleasure of the court?
Sound drums and trumpets! farewell sour annoy!
For here, I hope, begins our lasting joy.

Curtain.

THE END

Afterword

Many years ago I attended an exhibit of works by Robert Rauschenberg. One of them was a framed piece of hard-worn, heavy, yellowing drawing paper, nearly blank except for several large smudges and small dark spots. It was titled "Erased de Kooning Drawing."

Some years later it occurred to me that there were many worlds within the universe of Shakespeare's works. Why couldn't lines from the poems and plays be refashioned (borrowed, "appropriated," or "sampled,") for other dramatic uses?

The durable reign of Shakespeare suggests that the drawing power of his dramas lies in the language: the wit, fluency, acuity, and force of his verse and prose. The works—at least as they are performed—are distinguished and admired most for their language rather than for their characters, plots, or dramatic intensity. Indeed, though the characters and drama are virtually unmatched in the theater, it is the "poetry" (both verse and prose) that elevates them. Especially as the decades pass, the plots have come to seem serviceable but too contrived; they are no longer sufficient reason to stage the plays, but rather serve as the occasion for directors and actors to dramatize character through the rhetoric of the poetry. The pre-eminence of Shakespeare's language carries the day. Springing from the mouths of his many distinct characters, it gives voice to Shakespeare's genius—his insight into life and the human condition and his facility for expressing his innumerable keen observations, so that his collected work is praised through the ages for its universality.

So what about a play with dialogue that is all drawn from Shakespeare? A wholly new plot? A cast with names different than those used by Shakespeare? Different characterizations than his? Would lines lifted from Shakespeare and reshaped into dialogue serve, even elevate, a new story and characters in a drama that could stand on its own?

Partly to answer this last question, I composed *What's the Matter?* It is a collaboration between me and Shakespeare—an experiment with the traditional. It is a kind of homage. Another reason I created the play is that both the notion and the endeavor were fun.

While driven by Shakespeare's language, *What's the Matter?* is also Shakespearean in its characterizations, story, and structure. It is an imitation of a Shakespeare play, re-using Shakespeare's writings to tell a story made to emulate a Renaissance drama. It is a "romance" in the sense that the late plays of Shakespeare are sometimes called romances—some bad things happen en route to a happy ending. It is not a farce or patchwork of well-known speeches or passages. Lines from Shakespeare's plays and poems take on a different life in the context of this completely new story with dynamic characters.

Many lines in *What's the Matter?* are not lifted verbatim from the original works; I allowed myself certain liberties to serve the new story. To begin, of course, I inserted or swapped new proper nouns where needed—the names of my characters and places. To suit the speaker and occasion, I changed pronouns, antecedents, and verb number and tense. I spliced many lines together; at times I substituted a single word in a line (but never a word that does not appear in the Concordance), all while trying to maintain iambic pentameter where verse was used instead of prose. Almost all the stage directions are mine.

The handicaps, of course, are that what happens in the plot and what the characters can say are constrained by the lines available in that vast universe I have posited within Shakespeare's writings. Even so, the difficult part was not constructing characters and a story, but deciding what great poetry to cut in order to trim the play down to its current length (as well as create an abridged version for production). Given the near-infinitely possible combinations of lines, material abounds for more new plots and characters.

What's the Matter? was written to be performed. People who like Shakespeare—specifically those who prefer attending plays, rather than reading them—have another entrée to the main attraction: the language. People who produce Shakespeare might have another opportunity to engage with the poetry and an addition to the repertoire, a Shakespearean novelty, if the poetry can vitalize a new story and cast of characters. For those who enjoy attending the plays for the wit and force, intimacy and reach, lyricism and grandeur of the dramatic poetry, my hope is that this wholesale appropriation of Shakespeare will provide a unique opportunity to be entertained by it.

A. K. Ludwig

www.ingramcontent.com/pod-product-compliance
Lightning Source LLC
Chambersburg PA
CBHW061726020426
42331CB00006B/1115